W9-CFI-288

BY JOAN DIDION

FICTION

Run River

Play It As It Lays

A Book of Common Prayer

Democracy

NONFICTION

Slouching Towards Bethlehem

The White Album

Salvador

Miami

Joan Didion

THE WHITE ALBUM

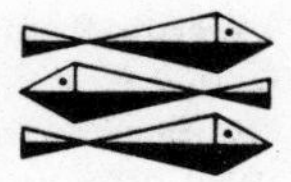

The Noonday Press

Farrar, Straus and Giroux

NEW YORK

Originally published in 1979 by Simon & Schuster
Printed in the United States of America
Published in Canada by HarperCollins*CanadaLtd*
Designed by Guy Fleming
This edition first published in 1990 by The Noonday Press

Library of Congress Cataloging-in-Publication Data
Didion, Joan.
The white album.
I. Title.
PS3554.I33W4 814'.5'4 79-10242

Most of these pieces appeared, in various forms and at various times, in the following magazines, and I would like to thank the editors of each: *Esquire, The Saturday Evening Post, Life* (more specifically, the "old" *Saturday Evening Post* and the "old" *Life*), *Travel & Leisure, The Los Angeles Times Book Review, The New York Times Book Review, New West,* and *The New York Review of Books*.

J.D.

Thanks are due the following publishers for permission to include excerpts from:

"Caracas I" from *Notebook* by Robert Lowell. Copyright © 1967, 1968, 1969, 1970 by Robert Lowell. Reprinted with the permission of Farrar, Straus & Giroux, Inc.

From Here to Eternity by James Jones. Copyright © 1951 by James Jones. Reprinted with the permission of Charles Scribner's Sons.

"California Winter" from *Collected Poems 1940–1978* by Karl Shapiro. Copyright © 1957 by Karl Shapiro. Reprinted with the permission of Wieser & Wieser, Inc., 118 East 25th St., New York, N.Y. 10010.

Lyric from "Moonlight Drive" by The Doors. Copyright © 1967 by Doors Music Company. Reprinted by permission.

For Earl McGrath,

and for Lois Wallace

Contents

IV / SOJOURNS

V / ON THE MORNING AFTER THE SIXTIES

I /

THE WHITE ALBUM

The White Album

1.

WE TELL OURSELVES STORIES in order to live. The princess is caged in the consulate. The man with the candy will lead the children into the sea. The naked woman on the ledge outside the window on the sixteenth floor is a victim of accidie, or the naked woman is an exhibitionist, and it would be "interesting" to know which. We tell ourselves that it makes some difference whether the naked woman is about to commit a mortal sin or is about to register a political protest or is about to be, the Aristophanic view, snatched back to the human condition by the fireman in priest's clothing just visible in the window behind her, the one smiling at the telephoto lens. We look for the sermon in the suicide, for the social or moral lesson in the murder of five. We interpret what we see, select the most workable of the multiple choices. We live entirely, especially if we are writers, by the imposition of a narrative line upon disparate images, by the "ideas" with which we have learned to freeze the shifting phantasmagoria which is our actual experience.

Or at least we do for a while. I am talking here about a time when I began to doubt the premises of all the stories I had ever told myself, a common condition but one I found troubling. I suppose this period began around 1966 and continued until 1971. During those five years I appeared, on the face of it, a competent enough member of some community or another, a signer of contracts and Air Travel cards, a citizen: I wrote a couple of times a month for one magazine or another, published two books, worked on several motion pictures; participated in the paranoia of the time, in the raising of a small child, and in the entertainment of large numbers of people passing through my house; made gingham curtains for spare bedrooms, remembered to ask agents if any reduction of points would be *pari passu* with the financing studio, put lentils to soak on Saturday night for lentil soup on Sunday, made quarterly F.I.C.A. payments and renewed my driver's license on time, missing on the written examination only the question about the financial responsibility of California drivers. It was a time of my life when I was frequently "named." I was named godmother to children. I was named lecturer and panelist, colloquist and conferee. I was even named, in 1968, a *Los Angeles Times* "Woman of the Year," along with Mrs. Ronald Reagan, the Olympic swimmer Debbie Meyer, and ten other California women who seemed to keep in touch and do good works. I did no good works but I tried to keep in touch. I was responsible. I recognized my name when I saw it. Once in a while I even answered letters addressed to me, not exactly upon receipt but eventually, particularly if the letters had come from strangers. "During my absence from the country these past eighteen months," such replies would begin.

This was an adequate enough performance, as improvisations go. The only problem was that my entire education, everything I had ever been told or had told myself, insisted that the production was never meant to be improvised: I was supposed to have a script, and had mislaid it. I was supposed to hear cues, and no longer did. I was meant to know the plot, but all I knew was what I saw: flash pictures in variable sequence, images with no "meaning" beyond their temporary arrangement, not a movie but a cutting-room experience. In what would probably be the middle of my life I wanted still to believe in the narrative and in the narrative's intelligibility, but to know that one could change the sense with every cut was to begin to perceive the experience as rather more electrical than ethical.

During this period I spent what were for me the usual proportions of time in Los Angeles and New York and Sacramento. I spent what seemed to many people I knew an eccentric amount of time in Honolulu, the particular aspect of which lent me the illusion that I could any minute order from room service a revisionist theory of my own history, garnished with a vanda orchid. I watched Robert Kennedy's funeral on a verandah at the Royal Hawaiian Hotel in Honolulu, and also the first reports from My Lai. I reread all of George Orwell on the Royal Hawaiian Beach, and I also read, in the papers that came one day late from the mainland, the story of Betty Lansdown Fouquet, a 26-year-old woman with faded blond hair who put her five-year-old daughter out to die on the center divider of Interstate 5 some miles south of the last Bakersfield exit. The child, whose fingers had to be pried loose from the Cyclone fence when she was rescued twelve hours later by the California Highway Patrol, reported that she had run after the car carrying her mother and stepfather and brother and sister for "a long time." Certain of these images did not fit into any narrative I knew.

Another flash cut:

"In June of this year patient experienced an attack of vertigo, nausea, and a feeling that she was going to pass out. A thorough medical evaluation elicited no positive findings and she was placed on Elavil, Mg 20, tid. . . . The Rorschach record is interpreted as describing a personality in process of deterioration with abundant signs of failing defenses and increasing inability of the ego to mediate the world of reality and to cope with normal stress. . . . Emotionally, patient has alienated herself almost entirely from the world of other human beings. Her fantasy life appears to have been virtually completely preempted by primitive, regressive libidinal preoccupations many of which are distorted and bizarre. . . . In a technical sense basic affective controls appear to be intact but it is equally clear that they are insecurely and tenuously maintained for the present by a variety of defense mechanisms including intellectualization, obsessive-compulsive devices, projection, reaction-formation, and somatization, all of which now seem inadequate to their task of controlling or containing an underlying psychotic process and are therefore in process of failure. The content of patient's responses is highly unconventional and frequently bizarre, filled with sexual and anatomical preoccupations, and basic reality contact is obviously and seriously impaired at times. In quality and level of sophistication patient's responses are characteristic of those of individuals of high average or superior intelligence but she is now functioning intellectually in impaired fashion at barely average level. Patient's thematic productions on the Thematic Apperception Test emphasize her fundamentally pessimistic, fatalistic, and depressive view of the world around her. It is as though she feels deeply that all human effort is foredoomed to failure, a conviction which seems to push her further

into a dependent, passive withdrawal. In her view she lives in a world of people moved by strange, conflicted, poorly comprehended, and, above all, devious motivations which commit them inevitably to conflict and failure . . ."

The patient to whom this psychiatric report refers is me. The tests mentioned—the Rorschach, the Thematic Apperception Test, the Sentence Completion Test and the Minnesota Multiphasic Personality Index—were administered privately, in the outpatient psychiatric clinic at St. John's Hospital in Santa Monica, in the summer of 1968, shortly after I suffered the "attack of vertigo and nausea" mentioned in the first sentence and shortly before I was named a *Los Angeles Times* "Woman of the Year." By way of comment I offer only that an attack of vertigo and nausea does not now seem to me an inappropriate response to the summer of 1968.

2.

In the years I am talking about I was living in a large house in a part of Hollywood that had once been expensive and was now described by one of my acquaintances as a "senseless-killing neighborhood." This house on Franklin Avenue was rented, and paint peeled inside and out, and pipes broke and window sashes crumbled and the tennis court had not been rolled since 1933, but the rooms were many and high-ceilinged and, during the five years that I lived there, even the rather sinistral inertia of the neighborhood tended to suggest that I should live in the house indefinitely.

In fact I could not, because the owners were

waiting only for a zoning change to tear the house down and build a high-rise apartment building, and for that matter it was precisely this anticipation of imminent but not exactly immediate destruction that lent the neighborhood its particular character. The house across the street had been built for one of the Talmadge sisters, had been the Japanese consulate in 1941, and was now, although boarded up, occupied by a number of unrelated adults who seemed to constitute some kind of therapy group. The house next door was owned by Synanon. I recall looking at a house around the corner with a rental sign on it: this house had once been the Canadian consulate, had 28 large rooms and two refrigerated fur closets, and could be rented, in the spirit of the neighborhood, only on a month-to-month basis, unfurnished. Since the inclination to rent an unfurnished 28-room house for a month or two is a distinctly special one, the neighborhood was peopled mainly by rock-and-roll bands, therapy groups, very old women wheeled down the street by practical nurses in soiled uniforms, and by my husband, my daughter and me.

Q. *And what else happened, if anything. . . .*

A. *He said that he thought that I could be a star, like, you know, a young Burt Lancaster, you know, that kind of stuff.*

Q. *Did he mention any particular name?*

A. *Yes, sir.*

Q. *What name did he mention?*

A. *He mentioned a lot of names. He said Burt Lancaster. He said Clint Eastwood. He said Fess Parker. He mentioned a lot of names. . . .*

Q. *Did you talk after you ate?*

A. *While we were eating, after we ate. Mr. Novarro told our fortunes with some cards and he read our palms.*

Q. *Did he tell you you were going to have a lot of good luck or bad luck or what happened?*

A. *He wasn't a good palm reader.*

These are excerpts from the testimony of Paul Robert Ferguson and Thomas Scott Ferguson, brothers, ages 22 and 17 respectively, during their trial for the murder of Ramon Novarro, age 69, at his house in Laurel Canyon, not too far from my house in Hollywood, on the night of October 30, 1968. I followed this trial quite closely, clipping reports from the newspapers and later borrowing a transcript from one of the defense attorneys. The younger of the brothers, "Tommy Scott" Ferguson, whose girl friend testified that she had stopped being in love with him "about two weeks after Grand Jury," said that he had been unaware of Mr. Novarro's career as a silent film actor until he was shown, at some point during the night of the murder, a photograph of his host as Ben-Hur. The older brother, Paul Ferguson, who began working carnivals when he was 12 and described himself at 22 as having had "a fast life and a good one," gave the jury, upon request, his definition of a hustler: "A hustler is someone who can talk—not just to men, to women, too. Who can cook. Can keep company. Wash a car. Lots of things make up a hustler. There are a lot of lonely people in this town, man." During the course of the trial each of the brothers accused the other of the murder. Both were convicted. I read the transcript several times, trying to bring the picture into some focus which did not suggest that I lived, as my psychiatric report had put it, "in a world of people moved by strange, conflicted, poorly comprehended and, above all, devious motivations"; I never met the Ferguson brothers.

I did meet one of the principals in another Los Angeles County murder trial during those years: Linda Kasabian, star witness for the prosecution in what was commonly known as the Manson Trial. I once asked Linda what she thought about the apparently chance sequence of events which had brought her first to the Spahn Movie Ranch and then to the Sybil Brand Institute for Women on charges, later dropped, of murdering Sharon Tate Polanski, Abigail Folger, Jay Sebring, Voytek Frykowski, Steven Parent, and Rosemary and Leno LaBianca. "Everything was to teach me something," Linda said. Linda did not believe that chance was without pattern. Linda operated on what I later recognized as dice theory, and so, during the years I am talking about, did I.

It will perhaps suggest the mood of those years if I tell you that during them I could not visit my mother-in-law without averting my eyes from a framed verse, a "house blessing," which hung in a hallway of her house in West Hartford, Connecticut.

God bless the corners of this house,
And be the lintel blest—
And bless the hearth and bless the board
And bless each place of rest—
And bless the crystal windowpane that lets the starlight in
And bless each door that opens wide, to stranger as to kin.

This verse had on me the effect of a physical chill, so insistently did it seem the kind of "ironic" detail the reporters would seize upon, the morning the bodies were found. In my neighborhood in California we did not bless the door that opened wide to stranger as to kin. Paul and Tommy Scott Ferguson were the strangers at Ramon Novarro's door, up on Laurel Canyon. Charles Manson was the stranger at Rosemary and Leno LaBianca's door, over in Los Feliz. Some strangers at the door knocked, and invented a reason to come inside: a call, say, to the Triple A, about a car not in evidence. Others just opened the door and walked in, and I would come across them in the entrance hall. I recall asking one such stranger what he wanted. We looked at each other for what seemed a long time, and then he saw my husband on the stair landing. "Chicken Delight," he said finally, but we had ordered no Chicken Delight, nor was he carrying any. I took the license number of his panel truck. It seems to me now that during those years I was always writing down the license numbers of panel trucks, panel trucks circling the block, panel trucks parked across the street, panel trucks idling at the intersection. I put these license numbers in a dressing-table drawer where they could be found by the police when the time came.

That the time would come I never doubted, at least not in the inaccessible places of the mind where I seemed more and more to be living. So many encounters in those years were devoid of any logic save that of the dreamwork. In the big house on Franklin Avenue many people seemed to come and go without relation to what I did. I knew where the sheets and towels were kept but I did not always know who was sleeping in every bed. I had the keys but not the key. I remember taking a 25-mg. Compazine one Easter Sunday and making a large and elaborate lunch for a number of people, many of whom were still around on Monday. I remember walking barefoot all day on the worn hardwood floors of that house and I remember "Do You Wanna Dance" on the record player, "Do You Wanna Dance" and "Visions of Johanna" and a song called "Midnight Confessions." I remember a babysitter telling me that she saw death in my aura. I remember chatting with her about reasons why this might be so, paying her, opening all the French windows and going to sleep in the living room.

It was hard to surprise me in those years. It was hard to even get my attention. I was absorbed in my intellectualization, my obsessive-compulsive devices, my projection, my reaction-formation, my somatization, and in the transcript of the Ferguson trial. A musician I had met a few years before called from a Ramada Inn in Tuscaloosa to tell me how to save myself through Scientology. I had met him once in my life, had talked to him for maybe half an hour about brown rice and the charts, and now he was telling me from Alabama about E-meters, and how I might become a Clear. I received a telephone call from a stranger in Montreal who seemed to want to enlist me in a narcotics operation. "Is it cool to talk on this telephone?" he asked several times. "Big Brother isn't listening?"

I said that I doubted it, although increasingly I did not.

"Because what we're talking about, basically, is applying the Zen philosophy to money and business, dig? And if I say we are going to finance the underground, and if I mention major money, you know what I'm talking about because you know what's going down, right?"

Maybe he was not talking about narcotics. Maybe he was talking about turning a profit on M-1 rifles: I had stopped looking for the logic in such calls. Someone with whom I had gone to school in Sacramento and had last seen in 1952 turned up at my house in Hollywood in 1968 in the guise of a private detective from West Covina, one of very few licensed women private detectives in the State of California. "They call us Dickless Tracys," she said, idly but definitely fanning out the day's mail on the hall table. "I have a lot of very close friends in law enforcement," she said then. "You might want to meet them." We exchanged promises to keep in touch but never met again: a not atypical encounter of the period. The Sixties were over before it occurred to me that this visit might have been less than entirely social.

3.

It was six, seven o'clock of an early spring evening in 1968 and I was sitting on the cold vinyl floor of a sound studio on Sunset Boulevard, watching a band called The Doors record a rhythm track. On the whole my attention was only minimally engaged by the preoccupations of rock-and-roll bands (I had already heard about acid as a transitional stage and also about the Maharishi and even about Universal Love, and after a while it all sounded like marmalade skies to me), but The Doors were different, The Doors interested me. The Doors seemed unconvinced that love was brotherhood and the Kama Sutra. The Doors' music insisted that love was sex and sex was death and therein lay salvation. The Doors were the Norman Mailers of the Top Forty, missionaries of apocalyptic sex. *Break on through,* their lyrics urged, and *Light my fire,* and:

Come on baby, gonna take a little ride
Goin' down by the ocean side
Gonna get real close
Get real tight
Baby gonna drown tonight—
Goin' down, down, down.

On this evening in 1968 they were gathered together in uneasy symbiosis to make their third album, and the studio was too cold and the lights were too bright and there were masses of wires and banks of the ominous blinking electronic circuitry with which musicians live so easily. There were three of the four Doors. There was a bass player borrowed from a band called Clear Light. There were the producer and the engineer and the road manager and a couple of girls and a Siberian husky named Nikki with one gray eye and one gold. There were paper bags half filled with hard-boiled eggs and chicken livers and cheeseburgers and empty bottles of apple juice and California rosé. There was everything and everybody The Doors needed to cut the rest of this third album except one thing, the fourth Door, the lead singer, Jim Morrison, a 24-year-old graduate of U.C.L.A. who wore black vinyl pants and no underwear and tended to suggest some range of the possible just beyond a suicide pact. It was Morrison who had described The Doors as "erotic politicians." It was Morrison who had defined the group's interests as "anything about revolt, disorder, chaos, about activity that appears to have no meaning." It was Morrison who got arrested in Miami in December of 1967 for giving an "indecent" performance. It was Morrison who wrote most of The Doors' lyrics, the peculiar character of which was to reflect either an ambiguous paranoia or a quite unambiguous insistence upon the love-death as the ultimate high. And it was Morrison who was missing. It was Ray Manzarek and Robby Krieger and John Densmore who made The Doors sound the way they sounded, and maybe it was Manzarek and Krieger and Densmore who made seventeen out of twenty interviewees on *American Bandstand* prefer The Doors over all other bands, but it was Morrison who got up there in his black vinyl pants with no underwear and projected the idea, and it was Morrison they were waiting for now.

"Hey listen," the engineer said. "I was listening to an FM station on the way over here, they played three Doors songs, first they played 'Back Door Man' and then 'Love Me Two Times' and 'Light My Fire.' "

"I heard it," Densmore muttered. "I heard it."

"So what's wrong with somebody playing three of your songs?"

"This cat dedicates it to his family."

"Yeah? To his family?"

"To his family. Really crass."

Ray Manzarek was hunched over a Gibson keyboard. "You think *Morrison*'s going to come back?" he asked to no one in particular.

No one answered.

"So we can do some *vocals?*" Manzarek said.

The producer was working with the tape of the rhythm track they had just recorded. "I hope so," he said without looking up.

"Yeah," Manzarek said. "So do I."

My leg had gone to sleep, but I did not stand up; unspecific tensions seemed to be rendering everyone in the room catatonic. The producer played back the rhythm track. The engineer said that he wanted to do his deep-breathing exercises. Manzarek ate a hard-boiled egg. "Tennyson made a mantra out of his own name," he said to the engineer. "I don't know if he said 'Tennyson Tennyson Tennyson' or 'Alfred Alfred Alfred' or 'Alfred Lord Tennyson,' but anyway, he did it. Maybe he just said 'Lord Lord Lord ' "

"Groovy," the Clear Light bass player said. He was an amiable enthusiast, not at all a Door in spirit.

"I wonder what Blake said," Manzarek mused. "Too bad *Morrison*'s not here. *Morrison* would know."

It was a long while later. Morrison arrived. He had on his black vinyl pants and he sat down on a leather couch in front of the four big blank speakers and he closed his eyes. The curious aspect of Morrison's arrival was this: no one acknowledged it. Robby Krieger continued working out a guitar passage. John Densmore tuned his drums. Manzarek sat at the control console and twirled a corkscrew and let a girl rub his shoulders. The girl did not look at Morrison, although he was in her direct line of sight. An hour or so passed, and still no one had spoken to Morrison. Then Morrison spoke to Manzarek. He spoke almost in a whisper, as if he were wresting the words from behind some disabling aphasia.

"It's an hour to West Covina," he said. "I was thinking maybe we should spend the night out there after we play."

Manzarek put down the corkscrew. "Why?" he said.

"Instead of coming back."

Manzarek shrugged. "We were planning to come back."

"Well, I was thinking, we could rehearse out there."

Manzarek said nothing.

"We could get in a rehearsal, there's a Holiday Inn next door."

"We could do that," Manzarek said. "Or we could rehearse Sunday, in town."

"I guess so." Morrison paused. "Will the place be ready to rehearse Sunday?"

Manzarek looked at him for a while. "No," he said then.

I counted the control knobs on the electronic console. There were seventy-six. I was unsure in whose favor the dialogue had been resolved, or if it had been resolved at all. Robby Krieger picked at his guitar, and said that he needed a fuzz box. The producer suggested that he borrow one from the Buffalo Springfield, who were recording in the next studio. Krieger shrugged. Morrison sat down again on the leather couch and leaned back. He lit a match. He studied the flame awhile and then very slowly, very deliberately, lowered it to the fly of his black vinyl pants. Manzarek watched him. The girl who was rubbing Manzarek's shoulders did not look at anyone. There was a sense that no one was going to leave the room, ever. It would be some weeks before The Doors finished recording this album. I did not see it through.

4.

SOMEONE ONCE BROUGHT Janis Joplin to a party at the house on Franklin Avenue: she had just done a concert and she wanted brandy-and-Benedictine in a water tumbler. Music people never wanted ordinary drinks. They wanted sake, or champagne cocktails, or tequila neat. Spending time with music people was confusing, and required a more fluid and ultimately a more passive approach than I ever acquired. In the first place time was never of the essence: we would have dinner at nine unless we had it at eleven-thirty, or we could order in later. We would go down to U.S.C. to see the Living Theater if the limo came at the very moment when no one had just made a drink or a cigarette or an arrangement to meet Ultra Violet at the Montecito. In any case David Hockney was coming by. In any case Ultra Violet was not at the Montecito. In any case we would go down to U.S.C. and see the Living Theater tonight or we would see the Living Theater another night, in New York, or Prague. First we wanted sushi for twenty, steamed clams, vegetable vindaloo and many rum drinks with gardenias for our hair. First we wanted a table for twelve, fourteen at the most, although there might be six more, or eight more, or eleven more: there would never be one or two more, because music people did not travel in groups of "one" or "two." John and Michelle Phillips, on their way to the hospital for the birth of their daughter Chynna, had the limo detour into Hollywood in order to pick up a friend, Anne Marshall. This incident, which I often embroider in my mind to include an imaginary second detour, to the Luau for gardenias, exactly describes the music business to me.

5.

AROUND FIVE O'CLOCK on the morning of October 28, 1967, in the desolate district between San Francisco Bay and the Oakland estuary that the Oakland police call Beat 101A, a 25-year-old black militant named Huey P. Newton was stopped and questioned by a white police officer named John Frey, Jr. An hour later Huey Newton was under arrest at Kaiser Hospital in Oakland, where he had gone for emergency treatment of a gunshot wound in his stomach, and a few weeks later he was indicted by the Alameda County Grand Jury on charges of murdering John Frey, wounding another officer, and kidnapping a bystander.

In the spring of 1968, when Huey Newton was awaiting trial, I went to see him in the Alameda County Jail. I suppose I went because I was interested in the alchemy of issues, for an issue is what Huey Newton had by then become. To understand how that had happened you must first consider Huey Newton, who he was. He came from an Oakland family, and for a while he went to Merritt College. In October of 1966 he and a friend named Bobby Seale organized what they called the Black Panther Party. They borrowed the name from the emblem used by the Freedom Party in Lowndes County, Alabama, and, from the beginning, they defined themselves as a revolutionary political group. The Oakland police knew the Panthers, and had a list of the twenty or so Panther cars. I am telling you neither that Huey Newton killed John Frey nor that Huey Newton did not kill John Frey, for in the context of revolutionary politics Huey Newton's guilt or innocence was irrelevant. I am telling you only how Huey Newton happened to be in the Alameda County Jail, and why rallies were held in his name, demonstrations organized whenever he appeared in court. LET'S SPRING HUEY, the buttons read (fifty cents each), and here and there on the courthouse steps, among the Panthers with their berets and sunglasses, the chants would go up:

Get your M-
31.

'Cause baby we gonna
Have some fun.
BOOM BOOM. BOOM BOOM.

"Fight on, brother," a woman would add in the spirit of a good-natured amen. "Bang-bang."

Bullshit bullshit
Can't stand the game
White man's playing.
One way out, one way out.
BOOM BOOM. BOOM BOOM.

In the corridor downstairs in the Alameda County Courthouse there was a crush of lawyers and CBC correspondents and cameramen and people who wanted to "visit Huey."

"Eldridge doesn't mind if I go up," one of the latter said to one of the lawyers.

"If Eldridge doesn't mind, it's all right with me," the lawyer said. "If you've got press credentials."

"I've got kind of dubious credentials."

"I can't take you up then. *Eldridge* has got dubious credentials. One's bad enough. I've got a good working relationship up there, I don't want to blow it." The lawyer turned to a cameraman. "You guys rolling yet?"

On that particular day I was allowed to go up, and a *Los Angeles Times* man, and a radio newscaster. We all signed the police register and sat around a scarred pine table and waited for Huey Newton. "The only thing that's going to free Huey Newton," Rap Brown had said recently at a Panther rally in Oakland

Auditorium, "is gunpowder." "Huey Newton laid down his life for us," Stokely Carmichael had said the same night. But of course Huey Newton had not yet laid down his life at all, was just here in the Alameda County Jail waiting to be tried, and I wondered if the direction these rallies were taking ever made him uneasy, ever made him suspect that in many ways he was more useful to the revolution behind bars than on the street. He seemed, when he finally came in, an extremely likable young man, engaging, direct, and I did not get the sense that he had intended to become a political martyr. He smiled at us all and waited for his lawyer, Charles Garry, to set up a tape recorder, and he chatted softly with Eldridge Cleaver, who was then the Black Panthers' Minister of Information. (Huey Newton was still the Minister of Defense.) Eldridge Cleaver wore a black sweater and one gold earring and spoke in an almost inaudible drawl and was allowed to see Huey Newton because he had those "dubious credentials," a press card from *Ramparts*. Actually his interest was in getting "statements" from Huey Newton, "messages" to take outside; in receiving a kind of prophecy to be interpreted as needed.

"We need a statement, Huey, about the ten-point program," Eldridge Cleaver said, "so I'll ask you a question, see, and you answer it . . ."

"How's Bobby," Huey Newton asked.

"He's got a hearing on his misdemeanors, see . . ."

"I thought he had a felony."

"Well, that's another thing, the felony, he's also got a couple of misdemeanors . . ."

Once Charles Garry had set up the tape recorder Huey Newton stopped chatting and started lecturing, almost without pause. He talked, running the words together because he had said them so many times before, about "the American capitalistic-materialistic system" and "so-called free enterprise" and "the fight for the liberation of black people throughout the world." Every now and then Eldridge Cleaver would signal Huey Newton and say something like, "There are a lot of people interested in the Executive Mandate Number Three you've issued to the Black Panther Party, Huey. Care to comment?"

And Huey Newton would comment. "Yes. Mandate Number Three is this demand from the Black Panther Party speaking for the black community. Within the Mandate we admonish the racist police force . . ." I kept wishing that he would talk about himself, hoping to break through the wall of rhetoric, but he seemed to be one of those autodidacts for whom all things specific and personal present themselves as mine fields to be avoided even at the cost of coherence, for whom safety lies in generalization. The newspaperman, the radio man, they tried:

Q. *Tell us something about yourself, Huey, I mean your life before the Panthers.*

A. *Before the Black Panther Party my life was very similar to that of most black people in this country.*

Q. *Well, your family, some incidents you remember, the influences that shaped you—*

A. *Living in America shaped me.*

Q. *Well, yes, but more specifically—*

A. *It reminds me of a quote from James Baldwin: "To be black and conscious in America is to be in a constant state of rage."*

"To be black and conscious in America is to be in a constant state of rage," Eldridge Cleaver wrote in large letters on a pad of paper, and then he added: *"Huey P. Newton quoting James Baldwin."* I could see it emblazoned above the speakers' platform at a rally, imprinted on the letterhead of an ad hoc committee still unborn. As a matter of fact almost everything Huey Newton said had the ring of being a "quotation," a "pronouncement" to be employed when the need arose. I had heard Huey P. Newton On Racism ("The Black Panther Party is against racism"), Huey P. Newton On Cultural Nationalism ("The Black Panther Party believes that the only culture worth holding on to is revolutionary culture"), Huey P. Newton On White Radicalism, On Police Occupation of the Ghetto, On the European Versus the African. "The European started to be sick when he denied his sexual nature," Huey Newton said, and Charles Garry interrupted then, bringing it back to first principles. "Isn't it true, though, Huey," he said, "that racism got its start for *economic* reasons?"

This weird interlocution seemed to take on a life of its own. The small room was hot and the fluorescent light hurt my eyes and I still did not know to what extent Huey Newton understood the nature of the role in which he was cast. As it happened I had always appreciated the logic of the Panther position, based as it was on the proposition that political power began at the end of the barrel of a gun (exactly what gun had even been specified, in an early memorandum from Huey P. Newton: *"Army .45; carbine; 12-gauge Magnum shotgun with 18" barrel, preferably the brand of High Standard; M-16; .357 Magnum pistols; P-38"*), and I could appreciate as well the particular beauty in Huey Newton as "issue." In the politics of revolution everyone was expendable, but I doubted that Huey Newton's political sophistication extended to seeing himself that way: the value of a Scottsboro case is easier to see if you are not yourself the Scottsboro boy. "Is there anything else you want to ask Huey?" Charles Garry asked. There did not seem to be. The lawyer adjusted his tape recorder. "I've had a request, Huey," he said, "from a high-school student, a reporter on his school paper, and he wanted a statement from you, and he's going to call me tonight. Care to give me a message for him?"

Huey Newton regarded the microphone. There was a moment in which he seemed not to remember the name of the play, and then he brightened. "I would like to point out," he said, his voice gaining volume as the memory disks clicked, *high school, student, youth, message to youth,* "that America is becoming a very young nation . . ."

I heard a moaning and a groaning, and I went over and it was—this Negro fellow was there. He had been shot in the stomach and at the time he didn't appear in any acute distress and so I said I'd see, and I asked him if he was a Kaiser, if he belonged to Kaiser, and he said, "Yes, yes. Get a doctor. Can't you see I'm bleeding? I've been shot. Now get someone out here." And I asked him if he had his Kaiser card and he got upset at this and he said, "Come on, get a doctor out here, I've been shot." I said, "I see this, but you're not in any acute distress." . . . So I told him we'd have to check to make sure he was a member. . . . And this kind of upset him more and he called me a few nasty names and said, "Now get a doctor out here right now, I've been shot and I'm bleeding." And he took his coat off and his shirt and he threw it on the desk there and he said, "Can't you see all this blood?" And I said, "I see it." And it wasn't that much, and so I said, "Well, you'll have to sign our admission sheet before you can be seen by a doctor." And he said, "I'm not signing anything." And I said, "You cannot be seen by a doctor unless you sign the admission sheet," and he said, "I don't have to sign anything" and a few more choice words . . .

This is an excerpt from the testimony before the Alameda County Grand Jury of Corrine Leonard, the nurse in charge of the Kaiser Foundation Hospital emergency room in Oakland at 5:30 A.M. on October 28, 1967. The "Negro fellow" was of course Huey Newton, wounded that morning during the gunfire which killed John Frey. For a long time I kept a copy of this testimony pinned to my office wall, on the theory that it illustrated a collision of cultures, a classic instance of an historical outsider confronting the established order at its most petty and impenetrable level. This theory was shattered when I learned that Huey Newton was in fact an enrolled member of the Kaiser Foundation Health Plan, i.e., in Nurse Leonard's words, "a Kaiser."

6.

ONE MORNING in 1968 I went to see Eldridge Cleaver in the San Francisco apartment he then shared with his wife, Kathleen. To be admitted to this apartment it was necessary to ring first and then stand in the middle of Oak Street, at a place which could be observed clearly from the Cleavers' apartment. After this scrutiny the visitor was, or was not, buzzed in. I was, and I climbed the stairs to find Kathleen Cleaver in the kitchen frying sausage and Eldridge Cleaver in the living room listening to a John Coltrane record and a number of other people all over the apartment, people everywhere, people standing in doorways and people moving around in one another's peripheral vision and people making and taking telephone calls. "When can you move on that?" I would hear in the background, and "You can't bribe me with a dinner, man, those *Guardian* dinners are all Old Left, like a wake." Most of these other people were members of the Black Panther Party, but one of them, in the living room, was Eldridge Cleaver's parole officer. It seems to me that I stayed about an hour. It seems to me that the three of us—Eldridge Cleaver, his parole officer and I—mainly discussed the commercial prospects of *Soul on Ice,* which, it happened, was being published that day. We discussed the advance ($5,000). We discussed the size of the first printing (10,000 copies). We discussed the advertising budget and we discussed the bookstores in which copies were or were not available. It was a not unusual discussion between writers, with the difference that one of the writers had his parole officer there and the other had stood out on Oak Street and been visually frisked before coming inside.

7.

TO PACK AND WEAR:

2 skirts
2 jerseys or leotards
1 pullover sweater
2 pair shoes
stockings
bra
nightgown, robe, slippers

cigarettes
bourbon
bag with:
  shampoo
  toothbrush and paste
  Basis soap
  razor, deodorant
  aspirin, prescriptions, Tampax
  face cream, powder, baby oil

To Carry:
  mohair throw
  typewriter
  2 legal pads and pens
  files
  house key

This is a list which was taped inside my closet door in Hollywood during those years when I was reporting more or less steadily. The list enabled me to pack, without thinking, for any piece I was likely to do. Notice the deliberate anonymity of costume: in a skirt, a leotard, *and stockings,* I could pass on either side of the culture. Notice the mohair throw for trunk-line flights (i.e., no blankets) and for the motel room in which the air conditioning could not be turned off. Notice the bourbon for the same motel room. Notice the typewriter for the airport, coming home: the idea was to turn in the Hertz car, check in, find an empty bench, and start typing the day's notes.

It should be clear that this was a list made by someone who prized control, yearned after momentum, someone determined to play her role as if she had the script, heard her cues, knew the narrative. There is on this list one significant omission, one article I needed and never had: a watch. I needed a watch not during the day, when I could turn on the car radio or ask someone, but at night, in the motel. Quite often I would ask the desk for the time every half hour or so, until finally, embarrassed to ask again, I would call Los Angeles and ask my husband. In other words I had skirts, jerseys, leotards, pullover sweater, shoes, stockings, bra, nightgown, robe, slippers, cigarettes, bourbon, shampoo, toothbrush and paste, Basis soap, razor, deodorant, aspirin, prescriptions, Tampax, face cream, powder, baby oil, mohair throw, typewriter, legal pads, pens, files and a house key, but I didn't know what time it was. This may be a parable, either of my life as a reporter during this period or of the period itself.

8.

DRIVING A Budget Rent-A-Car between Sacramento and San Francisco one rainy morning in November of 1968 I kept the radio on very loud. On this occasion I kept the radio on very loud not to find out what time it was but in an effort to erase six words from my mind, six words which had no significance for me but which seemed that year to signal the onset of anxiety or fright. The words, a line from Ezra Pound's "In a Station of the Metro," were these: *Petals on a wet black bough*. The radio played "Wichita Lineman" and "I Heard It on the Grapevine." *Petals on a wet black bough*. Somewhere between the Yolo Causeway and Vallejo it occurred to me that during the course of any given week I met too many people who spoke favorably about bombing power stations. Somewhere between the Yolo Causeway and Vallejo it also occurred to me that the fright on this particular morning was going to present itself as an inability to drive this Budget Rent-A-Car across the Carquinas Bridge. *The Wichita Lineman was still on the job.* I closed my eyes and drove across the Carquinas Bridge, because I had appointments, because I was working, because I had promised to watch the revolution being made at San Francisco State College and because there was no place in Vallejo to turn in a Budget Rent-A-Car and because nothing on my mind was in the script as I remembered it.

9.

AT SAN FRANCISCO STATE COLLEGE on that particular morning the wind was blowing the cold rain in squalls across the muddied lawns and against the lighted windows of empty classrooms. In the days before there had been fires set and classes invaded and finally a confrontation with the San Francisco Police Tactical Unit, and in the weeks to come the campus would become what many people on it were pleased to call "a battlefield." The police and the Mace and the noon arrests would become the routine of life on the campus, and every night the combatants would review their day on television: the waves of students advancing, the commotion at the edge of the frame, the riot sticks flashing, the instant of jerky camera that served to suggest at what risk the film was obtained; then a cut to the weather map. In the beginning there had been the necessary "issue," the suspension of a 22-year-old instructor who happened as well to be Minister of Education for the Black Panther Party, but that issue, like most, had soon ceased to be the point in the minds of even the most dense participants. Disorder was its own point.

I had never before been on a campus in disorder, had missed even Berkeley and Columbia, and I suppose I went to San Francisco State expecting something other than what I found there. In some not at all trivial sense, the set was wrong. The very architecture of California state colleges tends to deny radical notions, to reflect instead a modest and hopeful vision of progressive welfare bureaucracy, and as I walked across the campus that day and on later days the entire San Francisco State dilemma—the gradual politicization, the "issues" here and there, the obligatory "Fifteen Demands," the continual arousal of the police and the outraged citizenry—seemed increasingly off-key, an instance of the *enfants terribles* and the Board of Trustees unconsciously collaborating on a wishful fantasy (Revolution on Campus) and playing it out in time for the six o'clock news. "Adjet-prop committee meeting in the Redwood Room," read a scrawled note on the cafeteria door one morning; only someone who needed very badly to be alarmed could respond with force to a guerrilla band that not only announced its meetings on the enemy's bulletin board but seemed innocent of the spelling, and so the meaning, of the words it used. "Hitler Hayakawa," some of the faculty had begun calling S. I. Hayakawa, the semanticist who had become the college's third president in a year and had incurred considerable displeasure by trying to keep the campus open. "*Eichmann,*" Kay Boyle had screamed at him at a rally. In just such broad strokes was the picture being painted in the fall of 1968 on the pastel campus at San Francisco State.

The place simply never seemed serious. The headlines were dark that first day, the college had been closed "indefinitely," both Ronald Reagan and Jesse Unruh were threatening reprisals; still, the climate inside the Administration Building was that of a musical comedy about college life. "No *chance* we'll be open tomorrow," secretaries informed callers. "Go skiing, have a good time." Striking black militants dropped in to chat with the deans; striking white radicals exchanged gossip in the corridors. "No interviews, no press," announced a student strike leader who happened into a dean's office where I was sitting; in the next moment he was piqued because no one had told him that a Huntley-Brinkley camera crew was on campus. "We can still plug into that," the dean said soothingly. Everyone seemed joined in a rather festive camaraderie, a shared jargon, a shared sense of moment: the future was no longer arduous and indefinite but immediate and programmatic, aglow with the prospect of problems to be "addressed," plans to be "implemented." It was agreed all around that the confrontations could be "a very healthy development," that maybe it took a shutdown "to get something done." The mood, like the architecture, was 1948 functional, a model of pragmatic optimism.

Perhaps Evelyn Waugh could have gotten it down exactly right: Waugh was good at scenes of industrious self-delusion, scenes of people absorbed in odd games. Here at San Francisco State only the black militants could be construed as serious: they were at any rate picking the games, dictating the rules, and taking what they could from what seemed for everyone else just an amiable evasion of routine, of institutional anxiety, of the tedium of the academic calendar. Meanwhile the administrators could talk about programs. Meanwhile the white radicals could see themselves, on an investment of virtually nothing, as urban guerrillas. It was working out well for everyone, this game at San

Francisco State, and its peculiar virtues had never been so clear to me as they became one afternoon when I sat in on a meeting of fifty or sixty SDS members. They had called a press conference for later that day, and now they were discussing "just what the format of the press conference should be."

"This has to be on our terms," someone warned. "Because they'll ask very leading questions, they'll ask *questions.*"

"Make them submit any questions in writing," someone else suggested. "The Black Student Union does that very successfully, then they just don't answer anything they don't want to answer."

"That's it, don't fall into their trap."

"Something we should stress at this press conference is *who owns the media.*"

"You don't think it's common knowledge that the papers represent corporate interests?" a realist among them interjected doubtfully.

"I don't think it's *understood.*"

Two hours and several dozen hand votes later, the group had selected four members to tell the press who owned the media, had decided to appear *en masse* at an opposition press conference, and had debated various slogans for the next day's demonstration. "Let's see, first we have 'Hearst Tells It Like It Ain't', then 'Stop Press Distortion'—that's the one there was some political controversy about. . . ."

And, before they broke up, they had listened to a student who had driven up for the day from the College of San Mateo, a junior college down the peninsula from San Francisco. "I came up here today with some Third World students to tell you that we're with you, and we hope you'll be with *us* when we try to pull off a strike next week, because we're really into it, we carry our motorcycle helmets all the time, can't think, can't go to class."

He had paused. He was a nice-looking boy, and fired with his task. I considered the tender melancholy of life in San Mateo, which is one of the richest counties per capita in the United States of America, and I considered whether or not the Wichita Lineman and the petals on the wet black bough represented the aimlessness of the bourgeoisie, and I considered the illusion of aim to be gained by holding a press conference, the only problem with press conferences being that the press asked questions. "I'm here to tell you that at College of San Mateo we're living like *revolutionaries*," the boy said then.

10.

We put "Lay Lady Lay" on the record player, and "Suzanne." We went down to Melrose Avenue to see the Flying Burritos. There was a jasmine vine grown over the verandah of the big house on Franklin Avenue, and in the evenings the smell of jasmine came in through all the open doors and windows. I made bouillabaisse for people who did not eat meat. I imagined that my own life was simple and sweet, and sometimes it was, but there were odd things going around town. There were rumors. There were stories. Everything was unmentionable but nothing was unimaginable. This mystical flirtation with the idea of "sin"—this sense that it was possible to go "too far," and that many people were doing it—was very much with us in Los Angeles in 1968 and 1969. A demented and seductive vortical tension was building in the community. The jitters were setting in. I recall a time when the dogs barked every night and the moon was always full. On August 9, 1969, I was sitting in the shallow end of my sister-in-law's swimming pool in Beverly Hills when she received a telephone call from a friend who had just heard about the murders at Sharon Tate Polanski's house on Cielo Drive. The phone rang many times during the next hour. These early reports were garbled and contradictory. One caller would say hoods, the next would say chains. There were twenty dead, no, twelve, ten, eighteen. Black masses were imagined, and bad trips blamed. I remember all of the day's misinformation very clearly, and I also remember this, and wish I did not: *I remember that no one was surprised.*

11.

WHEN I FIRST MET Linda Kasabian in the summer of 1970 she was wearing her hair parted neatly in the middle, no makeup, Elizabeth Arden "Blue Grass" perfume, and the unpressed blue uniform issued to inmates at the Sybil Brand Institute for Women in Los Angeles. She was at Sybil Brand in protective custody, waiting out the time until she could testify about the murders of Sharon Tate Polanski, Abigail Folger, Jay Sebring, Voytek Frykowski, Steven Parent, and Rosemary and Leno LaBianca, and, with her lawyer, Gary Fleischman, I spent a number of evenings talking to her there. Of these evenings I remember mainly my dread at entering the prison, at leaving for even an hour the infinite possibilities I suddenly perceived in the summer twilight. I remember driving downtown on the

Hollywood Freeway in Gary Fleischman's Cadillac convertible with the top down. I remember watching a rabbit graze on the grass by the gate as Gary Fleischman signed the prison register. Each of the half-dozen doors that locked behind us as we entered Sybil Brand was a little death, and I would emerge after the interview like Persephone from the underworld, euphoric, elated. Once home I would have two drinks and make myself a hamburger and eat it ravenously.

"Dig it," Gary Fleischman was always saying. One night when we were driving back to Hollywood from Sybil Brand in the Cadillac convertible with the top down he demanded that I tell him the population of India. I said that I did not know the population of India. "Take a guess," he prompted. I made a guess, absurdly low, and he was disgusted. He had asked the same question of his niece ("a college girl"), of Linda, and now of me, and none of us had known. It seemed to confirm some idea he had of women, their essential ineducability, their similarity under the skin. Gary Fleischman was someone of a type I met only rarely, a comic realist in a porkpie hat, a business traveler on the far frontiers of the period, a man who knew his way around the courthouse and Sybil Brand and remained cheerful, even jaunty, in the face of the awesome and impenetrable mystery at the center of what he called "the case." In fact we never talked about "the case," and referred to its central events only as "Cielo Drive" and "LaBianca." We talked instead about Linda's childhood pastimes and disappointments, her high-school romances and her concern for her children. This particular juxtaposition of the spoken and the unspeakable was eerie and unsettling, and made my notebook a litany of little ironies so obvious as to be of interest only to dedicated absurdists. An example: Linda dreamed of opening a combination restaurant-boutique and pet shop.

12.

CERTAIN ORGANIC DISORDERS of the central nervous system are characterized by periodic remissions, the apparent complete recovery of the afflicted nerves. What happens appears to be this: as the lining of a nerve becomes inflamed and hardens into scar tissue, thereby blocking the passage of neural impulses, the nervous system gradually changes its circuitry, finds other, unaffected nerves to carry the same messages. During the years when I found it necessary to revise the circuitry of my mind I discovered that I was no longer interested in whether the woman on the ledge outside the window on the sixteenth floor jumped or did not jump, or in why. I was interested only in the picture of her in my mind: her hair incandescent in the floodlights, her bare toes curled inward on the stone ledge.

In this light all narrative was sentimental. In this light all connections were equally meaningful, and equally senseless. Try these: on the morning of John Kennedy's death in 1963 I was buying, at Ransohoff's in San Francisco, a short silk dress in which to be married. A few years later this dress of mine was ruined when, at a dinner party in Bel-Air, Roman Polanski accidentally spilled a glass of red wine on it. Sharon Tate was also a guest at this party, although she and Roman Polanski were not yet married. On July 27, 1970, I went to the Magnin-Hi Shop on the third floor of I. Magnin in Beverly Hills and picked out, at Linda Kasabian's request, the dress in which she began her testimony about the murders at Sharon Tate Polanski's house on Cielo Drive. "Size 9 Petite," her instructions read. "Mini but not extremely mini. In velvet if possible. Emerald green or gold. Or: A Mexican peasant-style dress, smocked or embroidered." She needed a dress that morning because the district attorney, Vincent Bugliosi, had expressed doubts about the dress she had planned to wear, a long white homespun shift. "Long is for evening," he had advised Linda. Long was for evening and white was for brides. At her own wedding in 1965 Linda Kasabian had worn a white brocade suit. Time passed, times changed. Everything was to teach us something. At 11:20 on that July morning in 1970 I delivered the dress in which she would testify to Gary Fleischman, who was waiting in front of his office on Rodeo Drive in Beverly Hills. He was wearing his porkpie hat and he was standing with Linda's second husband, Bob Kasabian, and their friend Charlie Melton, both of whom were wearing long white robes. Long was for Bob and Charlie, the dress in the I. Magnin box was for Linda. The three of them took the I. Magnin box and got into Gary Fleischman's Cadillac convertible with the top down and drove off in the sunlight toward the freeway downtown, waving back at me. I believe this to be an authentically senseless chain of correspondences, but in the jingle-jangle morning of that summer it made as much sense as anything else did.

13.

I RECALL a conversation I had in 1970 with the manager of a motel in which I was staying near Pendleton, Oregon. I had been doing a piece for *Life* about the storage of VX and GB nerve gas at an Army arsenal in Umatilla County, and now I was done, and trying to check out of the motel. During the course of checking out I was asked this question by the manager, who was a Mormon: *If you can't believe you're going to heaven in your own body and on a first-name basis with all the members of your family, then what's the point of dying?* At that time I believed that my basic affective controls were no longer intact, but now I present this to you as a more cogent question than it might at first appear, a kind of koan of the period.

14.

ONCE I HAD a rib broken, and during the few months that it was painful to turn in bed or raise my arms in a swimming pool I had, for the first time, a sharp apprehension of what it would be like to be old. Later I forgot. At some point during the years I am talking about here, after a series of periodic visual disturbances, three electroencephalograms, two complete sets of skull and neck X-rays, one five-hour glucose tolerance test, two electromyelograms, a battery of chemical tests and consultations with two ophthalmologists, one internist and three neurologists, I was told that the disorder was not really in my eyes, but in my central nervous system. I might or might not experience symptoms of neural damage all my life. These symptoms, which might or might not appear, might or might not involve my eyes. They might or might not involve my arms or legs, they might or might not be disabling. Their effects might be lessened by cortisone injections, or they might not. It could not be predicted. The condition had a name, the kind of name usually associated with telethons, but the name meant nothing and the neurologist did not like to use it. The name was multiple sclerosis, but the name had no meaning. This was, the neurologist said, an exclusionary diagnosis, and meant nothing.

I had, at this time, a sharp apprehension not of what it was like to be old but of what it was like to open the door to the stranger and find that the stranger did indeed have the knife. In a few lines of dialogue in a neurologist's office in Beverly Hills, the improbable had become the probable, the norm: things which happened only to other people could in fact happen to me. I could be struck by lightning, could dare to eat a peach and be poisoned by the cyanide in the stone. The startling fact was this: my body was offering a precise physiological equivalent to what had been going on in my mind. "Lead a simple life," the neurologist advised. "Not that it makes any difference we know about." In other words it was another story without a narrative.

15.

MANY PEOPLE I know in Los Angeles believe that the Sixties ended abruptly on August 9, 1969, ended at the exact moment when word of the murders on Cielo Drive traveled like brushfire through the community, and in a sense this is true. The tension broke that day. The paranoia was fulfilled. In another sense the Sixties did not truly end for me until January of 1971, when I left the house on Franklin Avenue and moved to a house on the sea. This particular house on the sea had itself been very much a part of the Sixties, and for some months after we took possession I would come across souvenirs of that period in its history—a piece of Scientology literature beneath a drawer lining, a copy of *Stranger in a Strange Land* stuck deep on a closet shelf—but after a while we did some construction, and between the power saws and the sea wind the place got exorcised.

I have known, since then, very little about the movements of the people who seemed to me emblematic of those years. I know of course that Eldridge Cleaver went to Algeria and came home an entrepreneur. I know that Jim Morrison died in Paris. I know that Linda Kasabian fled in search of the pastoral to New Hampshire, where I once visited her; she also visited me in New York, and we took our children on the Staten Island Ferry to see the Statue of Liberty. I also know that in 1975 Paul Ferguson, while serving a life sentence for the murder of Ramon Novarro, won first prize in a PEN fiction contest and announced plans to "continue my writing." Writing had helped him, he said, to "reflect on experience and see what it means." Quite often I reflect on the big house in Hollywood, on "Midnight Confessions" and on Ramon Novarro and on the fact that Roman Polanski and I are godparents to the same child, but writing has not yet helped me to see what it means.

1968–1978

II /

CALIFORNIA REPUBLIC

James Pike, American

It is a curious and arrogantly secular monument, Grace Episcopal Cathedral in San Francisco, and it imposes its tone on everything around it. It stands directly upon the symbolic nexus of all old California money and power, Nob Hill. Its big rose window glows at night and dominates certain views from the Mark Hopkins and the Fairmont, as well as from Randolph and Catherine Hearst's apartment on California Street. In a city dedicated to the illusion that all human endeavor tends mystically west, toward the Pacific, Grace Cathedral faces resolutely east, toward the Pacific Union Club. As a child I was advised by my grandmother that Grace was "unfinished," and always would be, which was its point. In the years after World War I my mother had put pennies for Grace in her mite box but Grace would never be finished. In the years after World War II I would put pennies for Grace in my mite box but Grace would never be finished. In 1964 James Albert Pike, who had come home from St. John the Divine in New York and *The Dean Pike Show* on ABC to be Bishop of California, raised three million dollars, installed images of Albert Einstein, Thurgood Marshall and John Glenn in the clerestory windows, and, in the name of God (James Albert Pike had by then streamlined the Trinity, eliminating the Son and the Holy Ghost), pronounced Grace "finished." This came to my attention as an odd and unsettling development, an extreme missing of the point—at least as I had understood the point in my childhood—and it engraved James Albert Pike on my consciousness more indelibly than any of his previous moves.

What was one to make of him. Five years after he finished Grace, James Albert Pike left the Episcopal Church altogether, detailing his pique in the pages of *Look,* and drove into the Jordanian desert in a white Ford Cortina rented from Avis. He went with his former student and bride of nine months, Diane. Later she would say that they wanted to experience the wilderness as Jesus had. They equipped themselves for this mission with an Avis map and two bottles of Coca-Cola. The young Mrs. Pike got out alive. Five days after James Albert Pike's body was retrieved from a canyon near the Dead Sea a Solemn Requiem Mass was offered for him at the cathedral his own hubris had finished in San Francisco. Outside on the Grace steps the cameras watched the Black Panthers demonstrating to free Bobby Seale. Inside the Grace nave Diane Kennedy Pike and her two predecessors, Jane Alvies Pike and Esther Yanovsky Pike, watched the cameras and one another.

That was 1969. For some years afterward I could make nothing at all of this peculiar and strikingly "now" story, so vast and atavistic was my irritation with the kind of man my grandmother would have called "just a damn old fool," the kind of man who would go into the desert with the sappy Diane and two bottles of Coca-Cola, but I see now that Diane and the Coca-Cola are precisely the details which lift the narrative into apologue. James Albert Pike has been on my mind quite a bit these past few weeks, ever since I read a biography of him by William Stringfellow and Anthony Towne, *The Death and Life of Bishop Pike*, an adoring but instructive volume from which there emerges the shadow of a great literary character, a literary character in the sense that Howard Hughes and Whittaker Chambers were literary characters, a character so ambiguous and driven and revealing of his time and place that his gravestone in the Protestant Cemetery in Jaffa might well have read only *JAMES PIKE, AMERICAN.*

Consider his beginnings. He was the only child of an ambitious mother and an ailing father who moved from Kentucky a few years before his birth in 1913 to homestead forty acres of mesquite in Oklahoma. There had been for a while a retreat to a one-room shack in Alamogordo, New Mexico, there had been always the will of the mother to improve the family's prospects. She taught school. She played piano with a dance band, she played piano in a silent-movie theater. She raised her baby James a Catholic and she entered him in the Better Babies Contest at the Oklahoma State Fair and he took first prize, two years running. "I thought you would like that," she told his biographers almost sixty years later. "He started out a winner."

He also started out dressing paper dolls in priests' vestments. The mother appears to have been a woman of extreme determination. Her husband died when James was two. Six years later the widow moved to Los Angeles, where she devoted herself to maintaining a world in which nothing "would change James' life or thwart him in any way," a mode of upbringing which would show in the son's face and manner all his life. "Needless to say this has all been a bit tedious for me to relive," he complained when the question of his first divorce and remarriage seemed to stand between him and election as Bishop of California; his biography is a panoply of surprised petulance in the face of other people's attempts to "thwart" him by bringing up an old marriage or divorce or some other "long-dead aspect of the past."

In Los Angeles there was Hollywood High, there was Mass every morning at Blessed Sacrament on Sunset Boulevard. After Hollywood High there was college with the Jesuits, at Santa Clara, at least until James repudiated the Catholic Church and convinced his mother that she should do the same. He was eighteen at the time, but it was characteristic of both mother and son to have taken this adolescent "repudiation" quite gravely: they give the sense of having had no anchor but each other, and to have reinvented their moorings every day. After Santa Clara, for the freshly invented agnostic, there was U.C.L.A., then U.S.C., and finally the leap east. Back East. Yale Law. A job in Washington with the Securities and Exchange Commission. "You have to understand that he was very lonely in Washington," his mother said after his death. "He really wanted to come home. I wish he had." And yet it must have seemed to such a western child that he had at last met the "real" world, the "great" world, the world to beat. The world in which, as the young man who started out a winner soon discovered and wrote to his mother, "practically every churchgoer you meet in our level of society is Episcopalian, and an R.C. or straight Protestant is as rare as hen's teeth."

One thinks of Gatsby, coming up against the East. One also thinks of Tom Buchanan, and his vast carelessness. (Some 25 years later, in Santa Barbara, when the Bishop of California's mistress swallowed 55 sleeping pills, he appears to have moved her from his apartment into her own before calling an ambulance, and to have obscured certain evidence before she died.) One even thinks of Dick Diver, who also started out a winner, and who tried to embrace the essence of the American continent in Nicole as James Albert Pike would now try to embrace it in the Episcopal Church. *"Practically every churchgoer you meet in our level of society is Episcopalian."*

It is an American Adventure of Barry Lyndon, this Westerner going East to seize his future, equipped with a mother's love and with what passed in the makeshift moorage from which he came as a passion for knowledge. As evidence of this passion his third wife, Diane, would repeat this curious story: he "had read both the dictionary and the phone book from cover to cover by the time he was five, and a whole set of the Encyclopaedia Britannica before he was ten." Diane also reports his enthusiasm for the Museum of Man in Paris, which seemed to him to offer, in the hour he spent there, "a complete education," the "entire history of the human race . . . in summary form."

In summary form. One gets a sense of the kind of mindless fervor that a wife less rapt than Diane might find unhinging. In the late thirties, as Communion was about to be served at the first Christmas Mass of James Albert Pike's new career as an Episcopalian, his first wife, Jane, another transplanted Californian, is reported to have jumped up and run screaming from the church. There would have been nothing in the phone book to cover that, or in the Britannica either. Later he invented an ecclesiastical annulment to cover his divorce from Jane, although no such annulment was actually granted. "In his mind," his biographers explain, "the marriage was not merely a mistake, but a nullity in the inception." In his mind. He needed to believe in the annulment because he wanted to be Bishop of California. "At heart he was a Californian," a friend said. "He had grown up with the idea that San Francisco was it . . . he was obsessed with the idea of being Bishop of California. Nothing in heaven or hell could have stopped him." In his mind. "Tom and Gatsby, Daisy and Jordan and I, were all Westerners," as Nick Carraway said, "and perhaps we possessed some deficiency in common which made us subtly unadaptable to Eastern life."

In his mind. I recall standing in St. Thomas Church in New York one Monday morning in 1964 debating whether or not to steal a book by James Albert Pike, a pastoral tract called *If You Marry Outside Your Faith*. I had only a twenty-dollar bill and could not afford to leave it in the box but I wanted to read the book more closely, because a few weeks before I had in fact married a Catholic, which was what Bishop Pike seemed to have in mind. I had not been brought up to think it made much difference what I married, as long as I steered clear of odd sects where they didn't drink at the wedding (my grandmother was an Episcopalian only by frontier chance; her siblings were Catholics but there was no Catholic priest around the year she needed christening), and I was struck dumb by Bishop Pike's position, which appeared to be that I had not only erred but had every moral right and obligation to erase this error by regarding my marriage as null, and any promises I had made as invalid. In other words the way to go was to forget it and start over.

In the end I did not steal *If You Marry Outside Your Faith*, and over the years I came to believe that I had doubtless misread it. After considering its source I am no longer so sure. "Jim never cleaned up after himself," a friend notes, recalling his habit of opening a shirt and letting the cardboards lie where they fell, and this *élan* seems to have applied to more than his laundry. Here was a man who moved through life believing that he was entitled to forget it and start over, to shed women when they became difficult and allegiances when they became tedious and simply *move on*, dismissing those who quibbled as petty and "judgmental" and generally threatened by his superior and more dynamic view of human possibility. That there was an ambivalence and a speciousness about this moral frontiersmanship has not gone unnoticed, but in the rush to call the life "only human" I suspect we are overlooking its real interest, which is as social history. The man was a Michelin to his time and place. At the peak of his career James Albert Pike carried his peace cross (he had put away his pectoral cross for the duration of the Vietnam War, which outlived him) through every charlatanic thicket in American life, from the Center for the Study of Democratic Institutions to the Aspen Institute of Humanistic Studies to Spiritual Frontiers, which was at the time the Ford Foundation of the spirit racket. James Albert Pike was everywhere at the right time. He was in Geneva for *Pacem in Terris*. He was in Baltimore for the trial of the Catonsville Nine, although he had to be briefed on the issue in the car from the airport. He was in the right room at the right time to reach his son, Jim Jr., an apparent suicide on Romilar, via séance. The man kept moving. If death was troubling then start over, and reinvent it as "The Other Side." If faith was troubling then leave the Church, and reinvent it as "The Foundation for Religious Transition."

This sense that the world can be reinvented

smells of the Sixties in this country, those years when no one at all seemed to have any memory or mooring, and in a way the Sixties were the years for which James Albert Pike was born. When the man who started out a winner was lying dead in the desert his brother-in-law joined the search party, and prayed for the assistance of God, Jim Jr., and Edgar Cayce. I think I have never heard a more poignant trinity.

1976

Holy Water

Some of us who live in arid parts of the world think about water with a reverence others might find excessive. The water I will draw tomorrow from my tap in Malibu is today crossing the Mojave Desert from the Colorado River, and I like to think about exactly where that water is. The water I will drink tonight in a restaurant in Hollywood is by now well down the Los Angeles Aqueduct from the Owens River, and I also think about exactly where that water is: I particularly like to imagine it as it cascades down the 45-degree stone steps that aerate Owens water after its airless passage through the mountain pipes and siphons. As it happens my own reverence for water has always taken the form of this constant meditation upon where the water is, of an obsessive interest not in the politics of water but in the waterworks themselves, in the movement of water through aqueducts and siphons and pumps and forebays and afterbays and weirs and drains, in plumbing on the grand scale. I know the data on water projects I will never see. I know the difficulty Kaiser had closing the last two sluiceway gates on the Guri Dam in Venezuela. I keep watch on evaporation behind the Aswan in Egypt. I can put myself to sleep imagining the water dropping a thousand feet into the turbines at Churchill Falls in Labrador. If the Churchill Falls Project fails to materialize, I fall back on waterworks closer at hand—the tailrace at Hoover on the Colorado, the surge tank in the Tehachapi Mountains that receives California Aqueduct water pumped higher than water has ever been pumped before—and finally I replay a morning when I was seventeen years old and caught, in a military-surplus life raft, in the construction of the Nimbus Afterbay Dam on the American River near Sacramento. I remember that at the moment it happened I was trying to open a tin of anchovies with capers. I recall the raft spinning into the narrow chute through which the river had been temporarily diverted. I recall being deliriously happy.

I suppose it was partly the memory of that delirium that led me to visit, one summer morning in Sacramento, the Operations Control Center for the California State Water Project. Actually so much water is moved around California by so many different agencies that maybe only the movers themselves know on any given day whose water is where, but to get a general picture it is necessary only to remember that Los Angeles moves some of it, San Francisco moves some of it, the Bureau of Reclamation's Central Valley Project moves some of it and the California State Water Project moves most of the rest of it, moves a vast amount of it, moves more water farther than has ever been moved anywhere. They collect this water up in the granite keeps of the Sierra Nevada and they store roughly a trillion gallons of it behind the Oroville Dam and every morning, down at the Project's headquarters in Sacramento, they decide how much of their water they want to move the next day. They make this morning decision according to supply and demand, which is simple in theory but rather more complicated in practice. In theory each of the Project's five field divisions—the Oroville, the Delta, the San Luis, the San Joaquin and the Southern divisions—places a call to headquarters before nine A.M. and tells the dispatchers how much water is needed by its local water contractors, who have in turn based their morning estimates on orders from growers and other big users. A schedule is made. The gates open and close according to schedule. The water flows south and the deliveries are made.

In practice this requires prodigious coordination, precision, and the best efforts of several human minds and that of a Univac 418. In practice it might be necessary to hold large flows of water for power production, or to flush out encroaching salinity in the Sacramento-San Joaquin Delta, the most ecologically sensitive point on the system. In practice a sudden rain might obviate the need for a delivery when that delivery is already on its way. In practice what is being delivered here is an enormous volume of water, not quarts of milk or spools of thread, and it takes two days to move such a delivery down through Oroville into the Delta, which is the great pooling place for California water and has been for some years alive with electronic sensors and telemetering equipment and men blocking channels and diverting flows and shoveling fish away from the pumps. It takes perhaps another six days to move this same water down the California Aqueduct from the Delta to the Tehachapi and put it over the hill to Southern California. "Putting some over the hill" is what they say around the Project Operations Control Center when they want to indicate that they are pumping Aqueduct water from the floor of the San Joaquin Valley up and over the Tehachapi Mountains. "Pulling it down" is what they say when they want to indicate that they are lowering a water level somewhere in the system. They can put some over the hill by remote control from this room in Sacramento with its Univac and its big board and its flashing lights. They can pull down a pool in the San Joaquin by remote control from this room in Sacramento with its locked doors and its ringing alarms and its constant print-outs of data from sensors out there in the water itself. From this room in Sacramento the whole system takes on the aspect of a perfect three-billion-dollar hydraulic toy, and in certain ways it is. "LET'S START DRAINING QUAIL AT 12:00" was the 10:51 A.M. entry on the electronically recorded communications log the day I visited the Operations Control Center. "Quail" is a reservoir in Los Angeles County with a gross capacity of 1,636,018,000 gallons. "OK" was the response recorded in the log. I knew at that moment that I had missed the only vocation for which I had any instinctive affinity: I wanted to drain Quail myself.

Not many people I know carry their end of the conversation when I want to talk about water deliveries, even when I stress that these deliveries affect their lives, indirectly, every day. "Indirectly" is not quite enough for most people I know. This morning, however, several people I know were affected not "indirectly" but "directly" by the way the water moves. They had been in New Mexico shooting a picture, one sequence of which required a river deep enough to sink a truck, the kind with a cab and a trailer and fifty or sixty wheels. It so happened that no river near the New Mexico location was running that deep this year. The production was therefore moved today to Needles, California, where the Colorado River normally runs, depending upon releases from Davis Dam, eighteen to twenty-five feet deep. Now. Follow this closely: yesterday we had a freak tropical storm in Southern California, two inches of rain in a normally dry month, and because this rain flooded the fields and provided more irrigation than any grower could possibly want for several days, no water was ordered from Davis Dam.

No orders, no releases.

Supply and demand.

As a result the Colorado was running only seven feet deep past Needles today, Sam Peckinpah's desire for eighteen feet of water in which to sink a truck not being the kind of demand anyone at Davis Dam is geared to meet. The production closed down for the weekend. Shooting will resume Tuesday, providing some grower orders water and the agencies controlling the Colorado release it. Meanwhile many gaffers, best boys, cameramen, assistant directors, script supervisors, stunt drivers and maybe even Sam Peckinpah are waiting out the weekend in Needles, where it is often 110 degrees at five P.M. and hard to get dinner after eight. This is a California parable, but a true one.

I have always wanted a swimming pool, and never had one. When it became generally known a year or so ago that California was suffering severe drought, many people in water-rich parts of the country seemed obscurely gratified, and made frequent reference to Californians having to brick up their swimming pools. In fact a swimming pool requires, once it has been filled and the filter has begun its process of cleaning and recirculating the water, virtually no water, but the symbolic content of swimming pools has always been interesting: a pool is misapprehended as a trapping of affluence, real or pretended, and of a kind of hedonistic attention to the body. Actually a pool is, for many of us in the West, a symbol not of affluence but of order, of control over the uncontrollable. A pool is water, made available and useful, and is, as such, infinitely soothing to the western eye.

It is easy to forget that the only natural force over which we have any control out here is water, and that only recently. In my memory California summers were characterized by the coughing in the pipes that meant the well was dry, and California winters by all-night watches on rivers about to crest, by sandbagging, by dynamite on the levees and flooding on the first floor. Even now the place is not all that hospitable to extensive settlement. As I write a fire has been burning out of control for two weeks in the ranges behind the Big Sur coast. Flash floods last night wiped out all major roads into Imperial County. I noticed this morning a hairline crack in a living-room tile from last week's earthquake, a 4.4 I never felt. In the part of California where I now live aridity is the single most prominent feature of the climate, and I am not pleased to see, this year, cactus spreading wild to the sea. There will be days this winter when the humidity will drop to ten, seven, four. Tumbleweed will blow against my house and the sound of the rattlesnake will be duplicated a hundred times a day by dried bougainvillea drifting in my driveway. The apparent ease of California life is an illusion, and those who believe the illusion real live here in only the most temporary way. I know as well as the next person that there is considerable transcendent value in a river running wild and undammed, a river running free over granite, but I have also lived beneath such a river when it was running in flood, and gone without showers when it was running dry.

"The West begins," Bernard DeVoto wrote, "where the average annual rainfall drops below twenty inches." This is maybe the best definition of the West I have ever read, and it goes a long way toward explaining my own passion for seeing the water under control, but many people I know persist in looking for psychoanalytical implications in this passion. As a matter of fact I have explored, in an amateur way, the more obvious of these implications, and come up with nothing interesting. A certain external reality remains, and resists interpretation. The West begins where the average annual rainfall drops below twenty inches. Water is important to people who do not have it, and the same is true of control. Some fifteen years ago I tore a poem by Karl Shapiro from a magazine and pinned it on my kitchen wall. This fragment of paper is now on the wall of a sixth kitchen, and crumbles a little whenever I touch it, but I keep it there for the last stanza, which has for me the power of a prayer:

> *It is raining in California, a straight rain*
> *Cleaning the heavy oranges on the bough,*
> *Filling the gardens till the gardens flow,*
> *Shining the olives, tiling the gleaming tile,*
> *Waxing the dark camellia leaves more green,*
> *Flooding the daylong valleys like the Nile.*

I thought of those lines almost constantly on the morning in Sacramento when I went to visit the California State Water Project Operations Control Center. If I had wanted to drain Quail at 10:51 that morning, I wanted, by early afternoon, to do a great deal more. I wanted to open and close the Clifton Court Forebay intake gate. I wanted to produce some power down at the San Luis Dam. I wanted to pick a pool at random on the Aqueduct and pull it down and then refill it, watching for the hydraulic jump. I wanted to put some water over the hill and I wanted to shut down all flow from the Aqueduct into the Bureau of Reclamation's Cross Valley Canal, just to see how long it would take somebody over at Reclamation to call up and complain. I stayed as long as I could and watched the system work on the big board with the lighted checkpoints. The Delta salinity report was coming in on one of the teletypes behind me. The Delta tidal report was coming in on another. The earthquake board, which has been desensitized to sound its alarm (a beeping tone for Southern California, a high-pitched tone for the north) only for those earthquakes which register at least 3.0 on the Richter Scale, was silent. I had no further business in this room and yet I wanted to stay the day. I wanted to be the one, that day, who was shining the olives, filling the gardens, and flooding the daylong valleys like the Nile. I want it still.

1977

Many Mansions

THE NEW OFFICIAL RESIDENCE for governors of California, unlandscaped, unfurnished, and unoccupied since the day construction stopped in 1975, stands on eleven acres of oaks and olives on a bluff overlooking the American River outside Sacramento. This is the twelve-thousand-square-foot house that Ronald and Nancy Reagan built. This is the sixteen-room house in which Jerry Brown declined to live. This is the vacant house which cost the State of California one-million-four, not including the property, which was purchased in 1969 and donated to the state by such friends of the Reagans as Leonard K. Firestone of Firestone Tire and Rubber and Taft Schreiber of the Music Corporation of America and Holmes Tuttle, the Los Angeles Ford dealer. All day at this empty house three maintenance men try to keep the bulletproof windows clean and the cobwebs swept and the wild grass green and the rattlesnakes down by the river and away from the thirty-five exterior wood and glass doors. All night at this empty house the lights stay on behind the eight-foot chain-link fence and the guard dogs lie at bay and the telephone, when it rings, startles by the fact that it works. "Governor's Residence," the guards answer, their voices laconic, matter-of-fact, quite as if there were some phantom governor to connect. Wild grass grows where the tennis court was to have been. Wild grass grows where the pool and sauna were to have been. The American is the river in which gold was discovered in 1848, and it once ran fast and full past here, but lately there have been upstream dams and dry years. Much of the bed is exposed. The far bank has been dredged and graded. That the river is running low is of no real account, however, since one of the many peculiarities of the new Governor's Residence is that it is so situated as to have no clear view of the river.

It is an altogether curious structure, this one-story one-million-four dream house of Ronald and Nancy Reagan's. Were the house on the market (which it will probably not be, since, at the time it was costing a million-four, local real estate agents seemed to agree on $300,000 as the top price ever paid for a house in Sacramento County), the words used to describe it would be "open" and "contemporary," although technically it is neither. "Flow" is a word that crops up quite a bit when one is walking through the place, and so is "resemble." The walls "resemble" local adobe, but they are not: they are the same concrete blocks, plastered and painted a rather stale yellowed cream, used in so many supermarkets and housing projects and Coca-Cola bottling plants. The door frames and the exposed beams "resemble" native redwood, but they are not: they are construction-grade lumber of indeterminate quality, stained brown. If anyone ever moves in, the concrete floors will be carpeted, wall to wall. If anyone ever moves in, the thirty-five exterior wood and glass doors, possibly the single distinctive feature in the house, will be, according to plan, "draped." The bathrooms are small and standard. The family bedrooms open directly onto the nonexistent swimming pool, with all its potential for noise and distraction. To one side of the fireplace in the formal living room there is what is known in the trade as a "wet bar," a cabinet for bottles and glasses with a sink and a long vinyl-topped counter. (This vinyl "resembles" slate.) In the entire house there are only enough bookshelves for a set of the World Book and some Books of the Month, plus maybe three Royal Doulton figurines and a back file of *Connoisseur*, but there is $90,000 worth of other teak cabinetry, including the "refreshment center" in the "recreation room." There is that most ubiquitous of all "luxury features," a bidet in the master bathroom. There is one of those kitchens which seem designed exclusively for defrosting by microwave and compacting trash. It is a house built for a family of snackers.

And yet, appliances notwithstanding, it is hard to see where the million-four went. The place has been called, by Jerry Brown, a "Taj Mahal." It has been called a "white elephant," a "resort," a "monument to the colossal ego of our former governor." It is not exactly any of these things. It is simply and rather astonishingly an enlarged version of a very common kind of California tract house, a monument not to colossal ego but to a weird absence of ego, a case study in the architecture of limited possibilities, insistently and malevolently "democratic," flattened out, mediocre and "open" and as devoid of privacy or personal eccentricity as the lobby area in a Ramada Inn. It is the architecture of "background music," decorators, "good taste." I recall once interviewing Nancy Reagan, at a time when her husband was governor and the construction on this house had not yet begun. We drove down to the State Capitol Building that day, and Mrs. Reagan showed me how she had lightened and brightened offices there by replacing the old burnished leather on the walls with the kind of beige burlap then favored in new office buildings. I mention this because it was on my mind as I walked through the empty house on the American River outside Sacramento.

From 1903 until Ronald Reagan, who lived in a rented house in Sacramento while he was governor ($1,200 a month, payable by the state to a group of Reagan's friends), the governors of California lived in a large white Victorian Gothic house at 16th and H Streets in Sacramento. This extremely individual house, three stories and a cupola and the face of Columbia the Gem of the Ocean worked into the molding over every door, was built in 1877 by a Sacramento hardware merchant named Albert Gallatin. The state paid $32,500 for it in 1903 and my father was born in a house a block away in 1908. This part of town has since run to seed and small business, the kind of place where both Squeaky Fromme and Patricia Hearst could and probably did go about their business unnoticed, but the Governor's Mansion, unoccupied and open to the public as State Historical Landmark Number 823, remains Sacramento's premier example of eccentric domestic architecture.

As it happens I used to go there once in a while, when Earl Warren was governor and his daughter Nina was a year ahead of me at C. K. McClatchy Senior High School. Nina was always called "Honey Bear" in the papers and in *Life* magazine but she was called "Nina" at C. K. McClatchy Senior High School and she was called "Nina" (or sometimes "Warren") at weekly meetings of the Mañana Club, a local institution to which we both belonged. I recall being initiated into the Mañana Club one night at the old Governor's Mansion, in a ceremony which involved being blindfolded and standing around Nina's bedroom in a state of high apprehension about secret rites which never materialized. It was the custom for the members to hurl mild insults at the initiates, and I remember being dumbfounded to hear Nina, by my fourteen-year-old lights the most glamorous and unapproachable fifteen-year-old in America, characterize me as "stuck on herself." There in the Governor's Mansion that night I learned for the first time that my face to the world was not necessarily the face in my mirror. "No smoking on the third floor," everyone kept saying. "Mrs. Warren *said.* No smoking on the third floor *or else.*"

Firetrap or not, the old Governor's Mansion was at that time my favorite house in the world, and probably still is. The morning after I was shown the new "Residence" I visited the old "Mansion," took the public tour with a group of perhaps twenty people, none of whom seemed to find it as ideal as I did. "All those stairs," they murmured, as if stairs could no longer be tolerated by human physiology. "All those stairs," and "all that waste space." The old Governor's Mansion does have stairs and waste space, which is precisely why it remains the kind of house in which sixty adolescent girls might gather and never interrupt the real life of the household. The bedrooms are big and private and high-ceilinged and they do not open on the swimming pool and one can imagine reading in one of them, or writing a book, or closing the door and crying until dinner. The bathrooms are big and airy and they do not have bidets but they do have room for hampers, and dressing tables, and chairs on which to sit and read a story to a child in the bathtub. There are hallways wide and narrow, stairs front and back, sewing rooms, ironing rooms, secret rooms. On the gilt mirror in the library there is worked a bust of Shakespeare, a pretty fancy for a hardware merchant in a California farm town in 1877. In the kitchen there is no trash compactor and there is no "island" with the appliances built in but there are two pantries, and a nice old table with a marble top for rolling out pastry and making divinity fudge and chocolate leaves. The morning I took the tour our guide asked if anyone could think why the old table had a marble top. There were a dozen or so other women in the group, each of an age to have cooked unnumbered meals, but not one of them could think of a single use for a slab of marble in the kitchen. It occurred to me that we had finally evolved a society in which knowledge of a pastry marble, like a taste for stairs and closed doors, could be construed as "elitist," and as I left the Governor's Mansion I felt very like the heroine of Mary McCarthy's *Birds of America*, the one who located America's moral decline in the disappearance of the first course.

A guard sleeps at night in the old mansion, which has been condemned as a dwelling by the state fire marshal. It costs about $85,000 a year to keep guards at the new official residence. Meanwhile the current governor of California, Edmund G. Brown, Jr., sleeps on a mattress on the floor in the famous apartment for which he pays $275 a month out of his own $49,100 annual salary. This has considerable and potent symbolic value, as do the two empty houses themselves, most particularly the house the Reagans built on the river. It is a great point around the Capitol these days to have "never seen" the house on the river. The governor himself has "never seen" it. The governor's press secretary, Elisabeth Coleman, has "never seen" it. The governor's chief of staff, Gray Davis, admits to having seen it, but only once, when "Mary McGrory wanted to see it." This unseen house on the river is, Jerry Brown has said, "not my style."

As a matter of fact this is precisely the point about the house on the river—the house is not Jerry Brown's style, not Mary McGrory's style, *not our style* —and it is a point which presents a certain problem, since the house so clearly *is* the style not only of Jerry Brown's predecessor but of millions of Jerry Brown's constituents. Words are chosen carefully. Reasonable objections are framed. One hears about how the house is too far from the Capitol, too far from the Legislature. One hears about the folly of running such a lavish establishment for an unmarried governor and one hears about the governor's temperamental austerity. One hears every possible reason for not living in the house except the one that counts: it is the kind of house that has a wet bar in the living room. It is the kind of house that has a refreshment center. It is the kind of house in which one does not live, but there is no way to say this without getting into touchy and evanescent and finally inadmissible questions of taste, and ultimately of class. I have seldom seen a house so evocative of the unspeakable.

1977

The Getty

THE PLACE MIGHT HAVE BEEN commissioned by The Magic Christian. Mysteriously and rather giddily splendid, hidden in a grove of sycamores just above the Pacific Coast Highway in Malibu, a commemoration of high culture so immediately productive of crowds and jammed traffic that it can now be approached by appointment only, the seventeen-million-dollar villa built by the late J. Paul Getty to house his antiquities and paintings and furniture manages to strike a peculiar nerve in almost everyone who sees it. From the beginning, the Getty was said to be vulgar. The Getty was said to be "Disney." The Getty was even said to be Jewish, if I did not misread the subtext in "like a Beverly Hills nouveau-riche dining room" (*Los Angeles Times*, January 6, 1974) and "gussied up like a Bel-Air dining room" (*New York Times*, May 28, 1974).

The Getty seems to stir up social discomforts at levels not easily plumbed. To mention this museum in the more enlightened of those very dining rooms it is said to resemble is to invite a kind of nervous derision, as if the place were a local hoax, a perverse and deliberate affront to the understated good taste and general class of everyone at the table. The Getty's intricately patterned marble floors and walls are "garish." The Getty's illusionistic portico murals are "back lot." The entire building, an informed improvisation on a villa buried by mud from Vesuvius in 79 A.D. and seen again only dimly during some eighteenth-century tunneling around Herculaneum, is ritually dismissed as "inauthentic," although what "authentic" could mean in this context is hard to say.

Something about the place embarrasses people. The collection itself is usually referred to as "that kind of thing," as in "not even the best of that kind of thing," or "absolutely top-drawer if you like that kind of thing," both of which translate "not our kind of thing." The Getty's damask-lined galleries of Renaissance and Baroque paintings are distinctly that kind of thing, there being little in the modern temperament that responds immediately to popes and libertine babies, and so are the Getty's rather unrelenting arrangements of French furniture. A Louis XV writing table tends to please the modern eye only if it has been demystified by a glass of field flowers and some silver-framed snapshots, as in a Horst photograph for *Vogue*. Even the Getty's famous antiquities are pretty much that kind of thing, evoking as they do not their own period but the eighteenth- and nineteenth-century rage for antiquities. The sight of a Greek head depresses many people, strikes an unliberated chord, reminds them of books in their grandmother's parlor and of all they were supposed to learn and never did. This note of "learning" pervades the entire Getty collection. Even the handful of Impressionists acquired by Getty were recently removed from the public galleries, put away as irrelevant. The Getty collection is in certain ways unremittingly reproachful, and quite inaccessible to generations trained in the conviction that a museum is meant to be fun, with Calder mobiles and Barcelona chairs.

In short the Getty is a monument to "fine art," in the old-fashioned didactic sense, which is part of the problem people have with it. The place resists contemporary notions about what art is or should be or ever was. A museum is now supposed to kindle the untrained imagination, but this museum does not. A museum is now supposed to set the natural child in each of us free, but this museum does not. This was art acquired to teach a lesson, and there is also a lesson in the building which houses it: the Getty tells us that the past was perhaps different from the way we like to perceive it. Ancient marbles were not always attractively faded and worn. Ancient marbles once appeared just as they appear here: as strident, opulent evidence of imperial power and acquisition. Ancient murals were not always bleached and mellowed and "tasteful." Ancient murals once looked as they do here: as if dreamed by a Mafia don. Ancient fountains once worked, and drowned out that very silence we have come to expect and want from the past. Ancient bronze once gleamed ostentatiously. The old world was once discomfitingly new, or even nouveau, as people like to say about the Getty. (I have never been sure what the word "nouveau" can possibly mean in America, implying as it does that the speaker is gazing down six hundred years of rolled lawns.) At a time when all our public conventions remain rooted in a kind of knocked-down romanticism, when the celebration of natural man's capacity for moving onward and upward has become a kind of official tic, the Getty presents us with an illustrated lesson in classical doubt. The Getty advises us that not much changes. The Getty tells us that we were never any better than we are and will never be any better than we were, and in so doing makes a profoundly unpopular political statement.

The Getty's founder may or may not have had some such statement in mind. In a way he seems to have wanted only to do something no one else could or would do. In his posthumous book, *As I See It,* he advises us that he never wanted "one of those concrete-bunker-type structures that are the fad among museum architects." He refused to pay for any "tinted-glass-and-stainless-steel monstrosity." He assures us that he was "neither shaken nor surprised" when his villa was finished and "certain critics sniffed." He had "calculated the risks." He knew that he was flouting the "doctrinaire and elitist" views he believed endemic in "many Art World (or should I say Artsy-Craftsy?) quarters."

Doctrinaire and elitist. Artsy-craftsy. On the surface the Getty would appear to have been a case of he-knew-what-he-liked-and-he-built-it, a tax dodge from the rather louche world of the international rich, and yet the use of that word "elitist" strikes an interesting note. The man who built himself the Getty never saw it, although it opened a year and a half before his death. He seems to have liked the planning of it. He personally approved every paint sample. He is said to have taken immense pleasure in every letter received from anyone who visited the museum and liked it (such letters were immediately forwarded to him by the museum staff), but the idea of the place seems to have been enough, and the idea was this: here was a museum built not for those elitist critics but for "the public." Here was a museum that would be forever supported by its founder alone, a museum that need never depend on any city or state or federal funding, a place forever "open to the public and free of all charges."

As a matter of fact large numbers of people who do not ordinarily visit museums like the Getty a great deal, just as its founder knew they would. There is one of those peculiar social secrets at work here. On the whole "the critics" distrust great wealth, but "the public" does not. On the whole "the critics" subscribe to the romantic view of man's possibilities, but "the public" does not. In the end the Getty stands above the Pacific Coast Highway as one of those odd monuments, a palpable contract between the very rich and the people who distrust them least.

1977

Bureaucrats

THE CLOSED DOOR upstairs at 120 South Spring Street in downtown Los Angeles is marked OPERATIONS CENTER. In the windowless room beyond the closed door a reverential hush prevails. From six A.M. until seven P.M. in this windowless room men sit at consoles watching a huge board flash colored lights. "There's the heart attack," someone will murmur, or "we're getting the gawk effect." 120 South Spring is the Los Angeles office of Caltrans, or the California Department of Transportation, and the Operations Center is where Caltrans engineers monitor what they call "the 42-Mile Loop." The 42-Mile Loop is simply the rough triangle formed by the intersections of the Santa Monica, the San Diego and the Harbor freeways, and 42 miles represents less than ten per cent of freeway mileage in Los Angeles County alone, but these particular 42 miles are regarded around 120 South Spring with a special veneration. The Loop is a "demonstration system," a phrase much favored by everyone at Caltrans, and is part of a "pilot project," another two words carrying totemic weight on South Spring.

The Loop has electronic sensors embedded every half-mile out there in the pavement itself, each sensor counting the crossing cars every twenty seconds. The Loop has its own mind, a Xerox Sigma V computer which prints out, all day and night, twenty-second readings on what is and is not moving in each of the Loop's eight lanes. It is the Xerox Sigma V that makes the big board flash red when traffic out there drops below fifteen miles an hour. It is the Xerox Sigma V that tells the Operations crew when they have an "incident" out there. An "incident" is the heart attack on the San Diego, the jackknifed truck on the Harbor, the Camaro just now tearing out the Cyclone fence on the Santa Monica. "Out there" is where incidents happen. The windowless room at 120 South Spring is where incidents get "verified." "Incident verification" is turning on the closed-circuit TV on the console and watching the traffic slow down to see (this is "the gawk effect") where the Camaro tore out the fence.

As a matter of fact there is a certain closed-circuit aspect to the entire mood of the Operations Center. "Verifying" the incident does not after all "prevent" the incident, which lends the enterprise a kind of tranced distance, and on the day recently when I visited 120 South Spring it took considerable effort to remember what I had come to talk about, which was that particular part of the Loop called the Santa Monica Freeway. The Santa Monica Freeway is 16.2 miles long, runs from the Pacific Ocean to downtown Los Angeles through what is referred to at Caltrans as "the East-West Corridor," carries more traffic every day than any other freeway in California, has what connoisseurs of freeways concede to be the most beautiful access ramps in the world, and appeared to have been transformed by Caltrans, during the several weeks before I went downtown to talk about it, into a 16.2-mile parking lot.

The problem seemed to be another Caltrans "demonstration," or "pilot," a foray into bureaucratic terrorism they were calling "The Diamond Lane" in their promotional literature and "The Project" among themselves. That the promotional literature consisted largely of schedules for buses (or "Diamond Lane Expresses") and invitations to join a car pool via computer ("Commuter Computer") made clear not only the putative point of The Project, which was to encourage travel by car pool and bus, but also the actual point, which was to eradicate a central Southern California illusion, that of individual mobility, without anyone really noticing. This had not exactly worked out. "FREEWAY FIASCO," the *Los Angeles Times* was headlining page-one stories. "THE DIAMOND LANE: ANOTHER BUST BY CALTRANS." "CALTRANS PILOT EFFORT ANOTHER IN LONG LIST OF FAILURES." "OFFICIAL DIAMOND LANE STANCE: LET THEM HOWL."

All "The Diamond Lane" theoretically involved was reserving the fast inside lanes on the Santa Monica for vehicles carrying three or more people, but in practice this meant that 25 per cent of the freeway was reserved for 3 per cent of the cars, and there were other odd wrinkles here and there suggesting that Caltrans had dedicated itself to making all movement around Los Angeles as arduous as possible. There was for example the matter of surface streets. A "surface street" is anything around Los Angeles that is not a freeway ("going surface" from one part of town to another is generally regarded as idiosyncratic), and surface streets do not fall directly within the Caltrans domain, but now the engineer in charge of surface streets was accusing Caltrans of threatening and intimidating him. It appeared that Caltrans wanted him to create a "confused and congested situation" on his surface streets, so as to force drivers back to the freeway, where they would meet a still more confused and congested situation and decide to stay home, or take a bus. "We are beginning a process of deliberately making it harder for drivers to use freeways," a Caltrans director had in fact said at a transit conference some months before. "We are prepared to endure considerable public outcry in order to pry John Q. Public out of his car. . . . I would emphasize that this is a political decision, and one that can be reversed if the public gets sufficiently enraged to throw us rascals out."

Of course this political decision was in the name of the greater good, was in the interests of "environmental improvement" and "conservation of resources," but even there the figures had about them a certain Caltrans opacity. The Santa Monica normally carried 240,000 cars and trucks every day. These 240,000 cars and trucks normally carried 260,000 people. What Caltrans described as its ultimate goal on the Santa Monica was to carry the same 260,000 people, "but in 7,800 fewer, or 232,200 vehicles." The figure "232,200" had a visionary precision to it that did not automatically create confidence, especially since the only effect so far had been to disrupt traffic throughout the Los Angeles basin, triple the number of daily accidents on the Santa Monica, prompt the initiation of two lawsuits against Caltrans, and cause large numbers of Los Angeles County residents to behave, most uncharacteristically, as an ignited and conscious proletariat. Citizen guerrillas splashed paint and scattered nails in the Diamond Lanes. Diamond Lane maintenance crews expressed fear of hurled objects. Down at 120 South Spring the architects of the Diamond Lane had taken to regarding "the media" as the architects of their embarrassment, and Caltrans statements in the press had been cryptic and contradictory, reminiscent only of old communiqués out of Vietnam.

To understand what was going on it is perhaps necessary to have participated in the freeway experience, which is the only secular communion Los Angeles has. Mere driving on the freeway is in no way the same as participating in it. Anyone can "drive" on the freeway, and many people with no vocation for it do, hesitating here and resisting there, losing the rhythm of the lane change, thinking about where they came from and where they are going. Actual participants think only about where they are. Actual participation requires a total surrender, a concentration so intense as to seem a kind of narcosis, a rapture-of-the-freeway. The mind goes clean. The rhythm takes over. A distortion of time occurs, the same distortion that characterizes the instant before an accident. It takes only a few seconds to get off the Santa Monica Freeway at National-Overland, which is a difficult exit requiring the driver to cross two new lanes of traffic streamed in from the San Diego Freeway, but those few seconds always seem to me the longest part of the trip. The moment is dangerous. The exhilaration is in doing it. "As you acquire the special skills involved," Reyner Banham observed in an extraordinary chapter about the freeways in his 1971 *Los Angeles: The Architecture of Four Ecologies,* "the freeways become a special way of being alive . . . the extreme concentration required in Los Angeles seems to bring on a state of heightened awareness that some locals find mystical."

Indeed some locals do, and some nonlocals too. Reducing the number of lone souls careering around the East-West Corridor in a state of mechanized rapture may or may not have seemed socially desirable, but what it was definitely not going to seem was easy. "We're only seeing an initial period of unfamiliarity,"

I was assured the day I visited Caltrans. I was talking to a woman named Eleanor Wood and she was thoroughly and professionally grounded in the diction of "planning" and it did not seem likely that I could interest her in considering the freeway as regional mystery. "Any time you try to rearrange people's daily habits, they're apt to react impetuously. All this project requires is a certain rearrangement of people's daily planning. That's really all we want."

It occurred to me that a certain rearrangement of people's daily planning might seem, in less rarefied air than is breathed at 120 South Spring, rather a great deal to want, but so impenetrable was the sense of higher social purpose there in the Operations Center that I did not express this reservation. Instead I changed the subject, mentioned an earlier "pilot project" on the Santa Monica: the big electronic message boards that Caltrans had installed a year or two before. The idea was that traffic information transmitted from the Santa Monica to the Xerox Sigma V could be translated, here in the Operations Center, into suggestions to the driver, and flashed right back out to the Santa Monica. This operation, in that it involved telling drivers electronically what they already knew empirically, had the rather spectral circularity that seemed to mark a great many Caltrans schemes, and I was interested in how Caltrans thought it worked.

"Actually the message boards were part of a larger pilot project," Mrs. Wood said. "An ongoing project in incident management. With the message boards we hoped to learn if motorists would modify their behavior according to what we told them on the boards."

I asked if the motorists had.

"Actually no," Mrs. Wood said finally. "They didn't react to the signs exactly as we'd hypothesized they would, no. *But*. If we'd *known* what the motorist would do . . . then we wouldn't have needed a pilot project in the first place, would we."

The circle seemed intact. Mrs. Wood and I smiled, and shook hands. I watched the big board until all lights turned green on the Santa Monica and then I left and drove home on it, all 16.2 miles of it. All the way I remembered that I was watched by the Xerox Sigma V. All the way the message boards gave me the number to call for CAR POOL INFO. As I left the freeway it occurred to me that they might have their own rapture down at 120 South Spring, and it could be called Perpetuating the Department. Today the California Highway Patrol reported that, during the first six weeks of the Diamond Lane, accidents on the Santa Monica, which normally range between 49 and 72 during a six-week period, totaled 204. Yesterday plans were announced to extend the Diamond Lane to other freeways at a cost of $42,500,000.

1976

Good Citizens

1.

I WAS ONCE INVITED to a civil rights meeting at Sammy Davis, Jr.'s house, in the hills above the Sunset Strip. "Let me tell you how to get to Sammy's," said the woman to whom I was talking. "You turn left at the old Mocambo." I liked the ring of this line, summing up as it did a couple of generations of that peculiar vacant fervor which is Hollywood political action, but acquaintances to whom I repeated it seemed uneasy. Politics are not widely considered a legitimate source of amusement in Hollywood, where the borrowed rhetoric by which political ideas are reduced to choices between the good (equality is good) and the bad (genocide is bad) tends to make even the most casual political small talk resemble a rally. "Those who cannot remember the past are condemned to repeat it," someone said to me at dinner not long ago, and before we had finished our *fraises des bois* he had advised me as well that "no man is an island." As a matter of fact I hear that no man is an island once or twice a week, quite often from people who think they are quoting Ernest Hemingway. "What a sacrifice on the altar of nationalism," I heard an actor say about the death in a plane crash of the president of the Philippines. It is a way of talking that tends to preclude further discussion, which may well be its intention: the public life of liberal Hollywood comprises a kind of dictatorship of good intentions, a social contract in which actual and irreconcilable disagreement is as taboo as failure or bad teeth, a climate devoid of irony. "Those men are our unsung heroes," a quite charming and intelligent woman once said to me at a party in Beverly Hills. She was talking about the California State Legislature.

I remember spending an evening in 1968, a week or so before the California primary and Robert Kennedy's death, at Eugene's in Beverly Hills, one of the "clubs" opened by supporters of Eugene McCarthy. The Beverly Hills Eugene's, not unlike Senator McCarthy's campaign itself, had a certain *déjà vu* aspect to it, a glow of 1952 humanism: there were Ben Shahn posters on the walls, and the gesture toward a strobe light was nothing that might interfere with "good talk," and the music was not 1968 rock but the kind of jazz people used to have on their record players when everyone who believed in the Family of Man bought Scandinavian stainless-steel flatware and voted for Adlai Stevenson. There at Eugene's I heard the name "Erich Fromm" for the first time in a long time, and many other names cast out for the sympathetic magic they might work ("I saw the Senator in San Francisco, where I was with Mrs. Leonard Bernstein . . ."), and then the evening's main event: a debate between William Styron and the actor Ossie Davis. It was Mr. Davis' contention that in writing *The Confessions of Nat Turner* Mr. Styron had encouraged racism ("Nat Turner's love for a white maiden, I feel my country can become psychotic about this"), and it was Mr. Styron's contention that he had not. (David Wolper, who had bought the motion picture rights to *Nat Turner*, had already made his position clear: "How can anyone protest a book," he had asked in the trade press, "that has withstood the critical test of time since last October?") As the evening wore on, Mr. Styron said less and less, and Mr. Davis more and more ("So you might ask, why didn't *I* spend five years and write *Nat Turner?* I won't go into my reasons why, but . . ."), and James Baldwin sat between them, his eyes closed and his head thrown back in understandable but rather theatrical agony. Mr. Baldwin summed up: "If Bill's book does no more than what it's done tonight, it's a very important event." "Hear, hear," cried someone sitting on the floor, and there was general agreement that it had been a stimulating and significant evening.

Of course there was nothing crucial about that night at Eugene's in 1968, and of course you could tell me that there was certainly no harm and perhaps some good in it. But its curious vanity and irrelevance stay with me, if only because those qualities characterize so many of Hollywood's best intentions. Social problems present themselves to many of these people in terms of a scenario, in which, once certain key scenes are licked (the confrontation on the courthouse steps, the revelation that the opposition leader has an anti-Semitic past, the presentation of the bill of particulars to the President, a Henry Fonda cameo), the plot will proceed inexorably to an upbeat fade. Marlon Brando does not, in a well-plotted motion picture, picket San Quentin in vain: what we are talking about here is faith in a dramatic convention. Things "happen" in motion pictures. There is always a resolution, always a strong cause-effect dramatic line, and to perceive the world in those terms is to assume an ending for every social scenario. If Budd Schulberg goes into Watts and forms a Writers' Workshop, then "Twenty Young Writers" must emerge from it, because the scenario in question is the familiar one about how the ghetto teems with raw talent and vitality. If the poor people march on Washington and camp out, there to receive bundles of clothes gathered on the Fox lot by Barbra Streisand, then some good must come of it (the script here has a great many dramatic staples, not the least of them a sentimental notion of Washington as an open forum, *cf. Mr. Deeds Goes to Washington*), and doubts have no place in the story.

There are no bit players in Hollywood politics: everyone makes things "happen." As it happens I live in a house in Hollywood in which, during the late thirties and early fifties, a screenwriters' cell of the Communist Party often met. Some of the things that are in the house now were in it then: a vast Stalinist couch, the largest rag rug I have ever seen, cartons of *New Masses*. Some of the people who came to meetings in the house were blacklisted, some of them never worked again and some of them are now getting several hundred thousand dollars a picture; some of them are dead and some of them are bitter and most of them lead very private lives. Things did change, but in the end it was not they who made things change, and their enthusiasms and debates sometimes seem very close to me in this house. In a way the house suggests the particular vanity of perceiving social life as a problem to be solved by the good will of individuals, but I do not mention that to many of the people who visit me here.

2.

PRETTY NANCY REAGAN, the wife then of the governor of California, was standing in the dining room of her rented house on 45th Street in Sacramento, listening to a television newsman explain what he wanted to do. She was listening attentively. Nancy Reagan is a very attentive listener. The television crew wanted to watch her, the newsman said, while she was doing precisely what she would ordinarily be doing on a Tuesday morning at home. Since I was also there to watch her doing precisely what she would ordinarily be doing on a Tuesday morning at home, we seemed to be on the verge of exploring certain media frontiers: the television newsman and the two cameramen could watch Nancy Reagan being watched by me, or I could watch Nancy Reagan being watched by the three of them, or one of the cameramen could step back and do a *cinéma vérité* study of the rest of us watching and being watched by one another. I had the distinct sense that we were on the track of something revelatory, the truth about Nancy Reagan at 24 frames a second, but the television newsman opted to overlook the moment's peculiar essence. He suggested that we watch Nancy Reagan pick flowers in the garden. "That's something you might ordinarily do, isn't it?" he asked. "Indeed it is," Nancy Reagan said with spirit. Nancy Reagan says almost everything with spirit, perhaps because she was once an actress and has the beginning actress's habit of investing even the most casual lines with a good deal more dramatic emphasis than is ordinarily called for on a Tuesday morning on 45th Street in Sacramento. "Actually," she added then, as if about to disclose a delightful surprise, "actually, I really *do* need flowers."

She smiled at each of us, and each of us smiled back. We had all been smiling quite a bit that morning. "And then," the television newsman said thoughtfully, surveying the dining-room table, "even though you've got a beautiful arrangement right now, we could set up the pretense of your arranging, you know, the flowers."

We all smiled at one another again, and then Nancy Reagan walked resolutely into the garden, equipped with a decorative straw basket about six inches in diameter. "Uh, Mrs. Reagan," the newsman called after her. "May I ask what you're going to select for flowers?"

"Why, I don't know," she said, pausing with her basket on a garden step. The scene was evolving its own choreography.

"Do you think you could use rhododendrons?"

Nancy Reagan looked critically at a rhododendron bush. Then she turned to the newsman and smiled. "Did you know there's a Nancy Reagan rose now?"

"Uh, no," he said. "I didn't."

"It's awfully pretty, it's a kind of, of, a kind of coral color."

"Would the . . . the Nancy Reagan rose be something you might be likely to pick now?"

A silvery peal of laughter. "I could certainly *pick* it. But I won't be *using* it." A pause. "I *can* use the rhododendron."

"Fine," the newsman said. "Just fine. Now I'll ask a question, and if you could just be nipping a bud as you answer it . . ."

"Nipping a bud," Nancy Reagan repeated, taking her place in front of the rhododendron bush.

"Let's have a dry run," the cameraman said.

The newsman looked at him. "In other words, by a dry run, you mean you want her to fake nipping the bud."

"Fake the nip, yeah," the cameraman said. "Fake the nip."

3.

Outside the Miramar Hotel in Santa Monica a hard subtropical rain had been falling for days. It scaled still more paint from the faded hotels and rooming houses that front the Pacific along Ocean Avenue. It streamed down the blank windows of unleased offices, loosened the soft coastal cliffs and heightened the most characteristic Santa Monica effect, that air of dispirited abandon which suggests that the place survives only as illustration of a boom gone bankrupt, evidence of some irreversible flaw in the laissez-faire small-business ethic. In any imaginative sense Santa Monica seemed an eccentric place for the United States Junior Chamber of Commerce to be holding a national congress, but there they were, a thousand delegates and wives, gathered in the Miramar Hotel for a relentless succession of keynote banquets and award luncheons and prayer breakfasts and outstanding-young-men forums. Now it was the President's Luncheon and everyone was listening to an animated singing group called The New Generation and I was watching the pretty young wife of one delegate pick sullenly at her lunch. "Let someone else eat this slop," she said suddenly, her voice cutting through not only the high generalities of the occasion but The New Generation's George M. Cohan medley as well. Her husband looked away, and she repeated it. To my left another delegate was urging me to ask every man in the room how the Jaycees had changed his life. I watched the girl down the table and asked the delegate how the Jaycees had changed his life. "It saved my marriage and it built my business," he whispered. "You could find a thousand inspirational stories right here at this President's Luncheon." Down the table the young wife was sobbing into a pink napkin. The New Generation marched into "Supercalifragilisticexpialidocious." In many ways the Jaycees' 32nd Annual Congress of America's Ten Outstanding Young Men was a curious and troubling way to spend a few days in the opening weeks of 1970.

I suppose I went to Santa Monica in search of the abstraction lately called "Middle America," went to find out how the Jaycees, with their Couéistic emphasis on improving one's world and one's self simultaneously, had weathered these past several years of cultural shock. In a very real way the Jaycees have exemplified, usually so ingenuously that it was popular to deride them, certain ideas shared by almost all of the people in America's small cities and towns and by at least some of the people in America's large cities, ideas shared in an unexamined way even by those who laughed at the Jaycees' boosterism and pancake breakfasts and safe-driving Road-e-os. There was the belief in business success as a transcendent ideal. There was the faith that if one transforms oneself from an "introvert" into an "extrovert," if one learns to "speak effectively" and "do a job," success and its concomitant, spiritual grace, follow naturally. There was the approach to international problems which construed the underdeveloped world as a temporarily depressed area in need mainly of People-to-People programs. ("Word of Operation Brotherhood swept through the teeming masses of Asia like a fresh wind from the sea," reads a Jaycee report on one such program in the late Fifties.) If only because these ideas, these last rattles of Social Darwinism, had in fact been held in common by a great many people who never bothered to articulate them, I wondered what the Jaycees were thinking now, wondered what their mood might be at a time when, as their national president put it one day at the Miramar, "so much of America seems to be looking at the negative."

At first I thought I had walked out of the rain into a time warp: the Sixties seemed not to have happened. All these Jaycees were, by definition, between 21 and 35 years old, but there was a disquieting tendency among them to have settled foursquare into middle age. There was the heavy jocularity, the baroque rhetoric of another generation entirely, a kind of poignant attempt to circumnavigate social conventions that had in fact broken down in the Twenties. Wives were lovely and forbearing. Getting together for drinks was having a cocktail reception. Rain was liquid sunshine and the choice of a table for dinner was making an executive decision. They knew that this was a brave new world and they said so. It was time to "put brotherhood into action," to "open our neighborhoods to those of all colors." It was time to "turn attention to the cities," to think about youth centers and clinics and the example set by a black policeman-preacher in Philadelphia who was organizing a decency rally patterned after Miami's. It was time to "decry apathy."

The word "apathy" cropped up again and again, an odd word to use in relation to the past few years, and it was a while before I realized what it meant. It was not simply a word remembered from the Fifties, when most of these men had frozen their vocabularies: it was a word meant to indicate that not enough of "our kind" were speaking out. It was a cry in the wilderness, and this resolute determination to meet 1950 head-on was a kind of refuge. Here were some people who had been led to believe that the future was always a rational extension of the past, that there would ever be world enough and time for "turning attention," for "problems" and "solutions." Of course they would not admit their inchoate fears that the world was not that way any more. Of course they would not join the "fashionable doubters." Of course they would ignore the "pessimistic pundits." Late one afternoon I sat in the Miramar lobby, watching the rain fall and the steam rise off the heated pool outside and listening to a couple of Jaycees discussing student unrest and whether the "solution" might not lie in on-campus Jaycee groups. I thought about this astonishing notion for a long time. It occurred to me finally that I was listening to a true underground, to the voice of all those who have felt themselves not merely shocked but personally betrayed by recent history. It was supposed to have been their time. It was not.

1968–1970

Notes Toward a Dreampolitik

1.

Elder Robert J. Theobold, pastor of what was until October 12, 1968, the Friendly Bible Apostolic Church in Port Hueneme, California, is twenty-eight years old, born and bred in San Jose, a native Californian whose memory stream could encompass only the boom years; in other words a young man who until October 12, 1968, had lived his entire life in the nerve center of the most elaborately technological and media-oriented society in the United States, and so the world. His looks and to some extent his background are indistinguishable from those of a legion of computer operators and avionics technicians. Yet this is a young man who has remained immaculate of the constant messages with which a technological society bombards itself, for at the age of sixteen he was saved, received the Holy Spirit in a Pentecostal church. Brother Theobold, as the eighty-some members of his congregation call him, now gets messages only from the Lord, "forcible impressions" instructing him, for example, to leave San Jose and start a church in Port Hueneme, or, more recently, to lead his congregation on the 12th of October, 1968, from Port Hueneme to Murfreesboro, Tennessee, in order to avoid destruction by earthquake.

"We're leaving the 12th but I don't have any message that it's going to happen before the end of

1968," Brother Theobold told me one morning a few weeks before he and his congregation piled their belongings into campers and cars and left California for Tennessee. He was minding the children that morning, and his two-year-old walked around sucking on a plastic bottle while Brother Theobold talked to me and fingered the pages of a tooled-leather Bible. "This one minister I heard, he definitely said it would happen before the end of 1970, but as far as I'm concerned, the Lord has shown me that it's definitely coming but he hasn't shown me *when*."

I mentioned to Brother Theobold that most seismologists were predicting an imminent major earthquake on the San Andreas Fault, but he did not seem unduly interested: Brother Theobold's perception of the apocalypse neither began with nor depended upon the empirical. In a way the Pentecostal mind reveals itself most clearly in something like Brother Theobold's earthquake prophecy. Neither he nor the members of his congregation to whom I talked had ever been particularly concerned by reports in the newspapers that an earthquake was overdue. "Of course we'd *heard* of earthquakes," a soft-voiced woman named Sister Mosley told me. "Because the Bible mentions there'll be more and more toward the end of time." Nor was there any need to think twice about pulling up stakes and joining a caravan to a small town few of them had ever seen. I kept asking Brother Theobold how he had chosen Murfreesboro, and over and over he tried to tell me: he had "received a telephone call from a man there," or "God had directed this particular man to call on this particular day." The man did not seem to have made a direct entreaty to Brother Theobold to bring his flock to Tennessee, but there had been no question in Brother

Theobold's mind that God's intention was exactly that. "From the natural point of view I didn't care to go to Murfreesboro at all," he said. "We just bought this place, it's the nicest place we ever had. But I put it up to the Lord, and the Lord said *put it up for sale*. Care for a Dr. Pepper?"

We might have been talking in different languages, Brother Theobold and I; it was as if I knew all the words but lacked the grammar, and so kept questioning him on points that seemed to him ineluctably clear. He seemed to be one of those people, so many of whom gravitate to Pentecostal sects, who move around the West and the South and the Border States forever felling trees in some interior wilderness, secret frontiersmen who walk around right in the ganglia of the fantastic electronic pulsing that is life in the United States and continue to receive information only through the most tenuous chains of rumor, hearsay, haphazard trickledown. In the social conventions by which we now live there is no category for people like Brother Theobold and his congregation, most of whom are young and white and nominally literate; they are neither the possessors nor the dispossessed. They participate in the national anxieties only through a glass darkly. They teach their daughters to eschew makeup and to cover their knees, and they believe in divine healing, and in speaking in tongues. Other people leave towns like Murfreesboro, and they move into them. To an astonishing extent they keep themselves unviolated by common knowledge, by the ability to make routine assumptions; when Brother Theobold first visited Murfreesboro he was dumbfounded to learn that the courthouse there had been standing since the Civil War. "The *same building*," he repeated twice, and then he got out a snapshot as corroboration. In the interior wilderness no one is bloodied by history, and it is no coincidence that the Pentecostal churches have their strongest hold in places where Western civilization has its most superficial hold. There are more than twice as many Pentecostal as Episcopal churches in Los Angeles.

2.

THE SCENE is quite near the end of Roger Corman's 1966 *The Wild Angels,* which was the first and in many ways the classic exploitation bike movie. Here it is: the Angels, led by Peter Fonda, are about to bury one of their number. They have already torn up the chapel, beaten and gagged the preacher, and held a wake, during which the dead man's girl was raped on the altar and the corpse itself, propped up on a bench in full biker colors, dark goggles over the eyes and a marijuana cigarette between the lips, was made an object of necrophilia. Now they stand at the grave, and, uncertain how to mark the moment, Peter Fonda shrugs. "Nothing to say," he says.

What we have here is an obligatory bike-movie moment, the outlaw-hero embracing man's fate: I tell you about it only to suggest the particular mood of these pictures. Many of them are extraordinarily beautiful in their instinct for the real look of the American West, for the faded banners fluttering over abandoned gas stations and for the bleached streets of desert towns. These are the movies known to the trade as "programmers," and very few adults have ever seen one. Most of them are made for less than $200,000. They are shown in New York only occasionally. Yet for several years bike movies have constituted a kind of underground folk literature for adolescents, have located an audience and fabricated a myth to exactly express that audience's every inchoate resentment, every yearning for the extreme exhilaration of death. To die violently is "righteous," a flash. To keep on living, as Peter Fonda points out in *The Wild Angels*, is just to keep on paying rent. A successful bike movie is a perfect Rorschach of its audience.

I saw nine of them recently, saw the first one almost by accident and the rest of them with a notebook. I saw *Hell's Angels on Wheels* and *Hell's Angels '69*. I saw *Run Angel Run* and *The Glory Stompers* and *The Losers*. I saw *The Wild Angels*, I saw *Violent Angels*, I saw *The Savage Seven* and I saw *The Cycle Savages*. I was not even sure why I kept going. To have seen one bike movie is to have seen them all, so meticulously observed are the rituals of getting the bikers out of town and onto the highway, of "making a run," of terrorizing the innocent "citizens" and fencing with the Highway Patrol and, finally, meeting death in a blaze, usually quite a literal blaze, of romantic fatalism. There is always that instant in which the outlaw leader stands revealed as existential hero. There is always that "perverse" sequence in which the bikers batter at some psychic sound barrier, degrade the widow, violate the virgin, defile the rose and the cross alike, break on through to the other side and find, once there, "nothing to say." The brutal images glaze the eye. The senseless insouciance of all the characters in a world of routine stompings and casual death takes on a logic better left unplumbed.

I suppose I kept going to these movies because

there on the screen was some news I was not getting from *The New York Times.* I began to think I was seeing ideograms of the future. To watch a bike movie is finally to apprehend the extent to which the toleration of small irritations is no longer a trait much admired in America, the extent to which a nonexistent frustration threshold is seen not as psychopathic but as a "right." A biker is goaded on the job about the swastika on his jacket, so he picks up a wrench, threatens the foreman, and later describes the situation as one in which the foreman "got uptight." A biker runs an old man off the road: the old man was "in the way," and his subsequent death is construed as further "hassling." A nurse happens into a hospital room where a biker beats her unconscious and rapes her: that she later talks to the police is made to seem a betrayal, evidence only of some female hysteria, vindictiveness, sexual deprivation. Any girl who "acts dumb" deserves what she gets, and what she gets is beaten and turned out from the group. Anything less than instant service in a restaurant constitutes intolerable provocation, or "hassling": tear the place apart, leave the owner for dead, gangbang the waitress. Rev up the Harleys and ride.

To imagine the audience for whom these sentiments are tailored, maybe you need to have sat in a lot of drive-ins yourself, to have gone to school with boys who majored in shop and worked in gas stations and later held them up. Bike movies are made for all these children of vague "hill" stock who grow up absurd in the West and Southwest, children whose whole lives are an obscure grudge against a world they think they never made. These children are, increasingly, everywhere, and their style is that of an entire generation.

3.

Palms, California, is a part of Los Angeles through which many people drive on their way from 20th Century-Fox to Metro-Goldwyn-Mayer, and vice versa. It is an area largely unnoticed by those who drive though it, an invisible prairie of stucco bungalows and two-story "units," and I mention it at all only because it is in Palms that a young woman named Dallas Beardsley lives. Dallas Beardsley has spent all of her twenty-two years on this invisible underside of the Los Angeles fabric, living with her mother in places like Palms and Inglewood and Westchester: she went to Airport Junior High School, out near Los Angeles International Airport, and to Westchester High School, where she did not go out with boys but did try out for cheerleader. She remembers not being chosen cheerleader as her "biggest discouragement." After that she decided to become an actress, and one morning in October of 1968 she bought the fifth page of *Daily Variety* for an advertisement which read in part: "There is no one like me in the world. I'm going to be a movie star."

It seemed an anachronistic ambition, wanting to be a movie star; girls were not supposed to want that in 1968. They were supposed to want only to perfect their *karma*, to give and get what were called good vibrations and to renounce personal ambition as an ego game. They were supposed to know that wanting things leads in general to grief, and that wanting to be a movie star leads in particular to U.C.L.A. Neuropsychiatric. Such are our conventions. But here was Dallas Beardsley, telling the world what she wanted for $50 down and $35 a month on an eight-month contract with *Variety*. *I'm going to be a movie star.*

I called Dallas, and one hot afternoon we drove around the Hollywood hills and talked. Dallas had long blond hair and a sundress and she was concerned about a run in her stocking and she did not hesitate when I asked what it meant to be a movie star. "It means being known all over the world," she said. "And bringing my family a bunch of presents on Christmas Day, you know, like carloads, and putting them by the tree. And it means happiness, and living by the ocean in a huge house." She paused. "But being *known*. It's important to me to be *known*." That morning she had seen an agent, and she was pleased because he had said that his decision not to handle her was "nothing personal." "The big agents are nice," she said. "They answer letters, they return your calls. It's the little ones who're nasty. But I understand, I really do." Dallas believes that all people, even agents, are "basically good inside," and that "when they hurt you, it's because they've been hurt themselves, and anyway maybe God means for you to be hurt, so some beautiful thing can happen later." Dallas attends the Unity Church in Culver City, the general thrust of which is that everything works out for the best, and she described herself as "pretty religious" and "politically less on the liberal side than most actors."

Her dedication to the future is undiluted. The jobs she takes to support herself—she has been a Kelly Girl, and worked in restaurants—do not intrude upon her ambitions. She does not go out to parties or on dates. "I work till six-thirty, then I have a dance lesson, then I rehearse at the workshop—when would I have time? Anyway I'm not interested in that." As I drove home that day through the somnolent back streets of Hollywood I had the distinct sense that everyone I knew had some fever which had not yet infected the invisible city. In the invisible city girls were still disappointed at not being chosen cheerleader. In the invisible city girls still got discovered at Schwab's and later met their true loves at the Mocambo or the Troc, still dreamed of big houses by the ocean and carloads of presents by the Christmas tree, still prayed to be known.

4.

ANOTHER PART of the invisible city.

"Speaking for myself," the young woman said, "in this seven months since I been on the program it's been real good. I was strictly a Gardena player, lowball. I'd play in the nighttime after I got my children to bed, and of course I never got home before five A.M., and my problem was, I couldn't sleep then, I'd replay every hand, so the next day I'd be, you know, tired. Irritable. With the children."

Her tone was that of someone who had adapted her mode of public address from analgesic commercials, but she was not exactly selling a product. She was making a "confession" at a meeting of Gamblers Anonymous: nine o'clock on a winter evening in a neighborhood clubhouse in Gardena, California. Gardena is the draw-poker capital of Los Angeles County (no stud, no alcoholic beverages, clubs closed between five A.M. and nine A.M. and all day on Christmas Day), and the proximity of the poker clubs hung over this meeting like a paraphysical substance, almost as palpable as the American flag, the portraits of Washington and Lincoln, and the table laid by the Refreshments Committee. There it was, just around the corner, the action, and here in this overheated room were forty people, shifting uneasily on folding chairs and blinking against the cigarette smoke, who craved it. "I never made this Gardena meeting before," one of them said, "for one simple reason only, which is I break out in a cold sweat every time I pass Gardena on the freeway even, but I'm here tonight because every night I make a meeting is a night I don't place a bet, which with the help of God and you people is 1,223 nights now." Another: "I started out for a Canoga Park meeting and turned around on the freeway, that was last Wednesday, I ended up in Gardena and now I'm on the verge of divorce again." And a third: "I didn't lose no fortune, but I lost all the money I could get my hands on, it began in the Marine Corps, I met a lot of pigeons in Vietnam, I was making easy money and it was, you might say, this period in my life that, uh, led to my downfall." This last speaker was a young man who said that he had done OK in mechanical drawing at Van Nuys High School. He wore his hair in a sharp 1951 ducktail. He was, like Dallas Beardsley, twenty-two years old. Tell me the name of the elected representative from the invisible city.

1968–1970

III /

WOMEN

The Women's Movement

To make an omelette you need not only those broken eggs but someone "oppressed" to break them: every revolutionist is presumed to understand that, and also every woman, which either does or does not make fifty-one per cent of the population of the United States a potentially revolutionary class. The creation of this revolutionary "class" was from the virtual beginning the "idea" of the women's movement, and the tendency for popular discussion of the movement to center for so long around day-care centers is yet another instance of that studied resistance to political ideas which characterizes our national life.

"The new feminism is not just the revival of a serious political movement for social equality," the feminist theorist Shulamith Firestone announced flatly in 1970. "It is the second wave of the most important revolution in history." This was scarcely a statement of purpose anyone could find cryptic, and it was scarcely the only statement of its kind in the literature of the movement. Nonetheless, in 1972, in a "special issue" on women, *Time* was still musing genially that the movement might well succeed in bringing about "fewer diapers and more Dante."

That was a very pretty image, the idle ladies sitting in the gazebo and murmuring *lasciate ogni speranza*, but it depended entirely upon the popular view of the movement as some kind of collective inchoate yearning for "fulfillment," or "self-expression," a yearning absolutely devoid of ideas and capable of engendering only the most *pro forma* benevolent interest. In fact there was an idea, and the idea was Marxist, and it was precisely to the extent that there was this Marxist idea that the curious historical anomaly known as the women's movement would have seemed to have any interest at all. Marxism in this country had ever been an eccentric and quixotic passion. One oppressed class after another had seemed finally to miss the point. The have-nots, it turned out, aspired mainly to having. The minorities seemed to promise more, but finally disappointed: it developed that they actually cared about the issues, that they tended to see the integration of the luncheonette and the seat in the front of the bus as real goals, and only rarely as ploys, counters in a larger game. They resisted that essential inductive leap from the immediate reform to the social ideal, and, just as disappointingly, they failed to perceive their common cause with other minorities, continued to exhibit a self-interest disconcerting in the extreme to organizers steeped in the rhetoric of "brotherhood."

And then, at that exact dispirited moment when there seemed no one at all willing to play the proletariat, along came the women's movement, and the invention of women as a "class." One could not help admiring the radical simplicity of this instant transfiguration. The notion that, in the absence of a cooperative proletariat, a revolutionary class might simply be invented, made up, "named" and so brought into existence, seemed at once so pragmatic and so visionary, so precisely Emersonian, that it took the breath away, exactly confirmed one's idea of where nineteenth-century transcendental instincts, crossed with a late reading of Engels and Marx, might lead. To read the theorists of the women's movement was to think not of Mary Wollstonecraft but of Margaret Fuller at her most high-minded, of rushing position papers off to mimeo and drinking tea from paper cups in lieu of eating lunch; of thin raincoats on bitter nights. If the family was the last fortress of capitalism, then let us abolish the family. If the necessity for conventional reproduction of the species seemed unfair to women, then let us transcend, via technology, "the very organization of nature," the oppression, as Shulamith Firestone saw it, "that goes back through recorded history to the animal kingdom itself." *I accept the universe,* Margaret Fuller had finally allowed: Shulamith Firestone did not.

It seemed very New England, this febrile and cerebral passion. The solemn *a priori* idealism in the guise of radical materialism somehow bespoke old-fashioned self-reliance and prudent sacrifice. The clumsy torrent of words became a principle, a renunciation of style as unserious. The rhetorical willingness to break eggs became, in practice, only a thrifty capacity for finding the sermon in every stone. Burn the literature, Ti-Grace Atkinson said in effect when it was suggested that, even come the revolution, there would still remain the whole body of "sexist" Western literature. But of course no books would be burned: the women of this movement were perfectly capable of crafting didactic revisions of whatever apparently intractable material came to hand. "As a parent you should become an interpreter of myths," advised Letty Cottin Pogrebin in the preview issue of *Ms.* "Portions of any fairy tale or children's story can be salvaged during a critique session with your child." Other literary analysts devised ways to salvage other books: Isabel Archer in *The Portrait of a Lady* need no longer be the victim of her own idealism. She could be, instead, the victim of a sexist society, a woman who had "internalized the conventional definition of wife." The narrator of Mary McCarthy's *The Company She Keeps* could be seen as "enslaved because she persists in looking for her identity in a man." Similarly, Miss McCarthy's *The Group* could serve to illustrate "what happens to women who have been educated at first-rate women's colleges—taught philosophy and history—and then are consigned to breast-feeding and gourmet cooking."

The idea that fiction has certain irreducible ambiguities seemed never to occur to these women, nor should it have, for fiction is in most ways hostile to ideology. They had invented a class; now they had only to make that class conscious. They seized as a political technique a kind of shared testimony at first called a "rap session," then called "consciousness-raising," and in any case a therapeutically oriented American reinterpretation, according to the British feminist Juliet Mitchell, of a Chinese revolutionary practice known as "speaking bitterness." They purged and regrouped and purged again, worried out one another's errors and deviations, the "elitism" here, the "careerism" there. It would have been merely sententious to call some of their thinking Stalinist: of course it was. It would have been pointless even to speak of whether one considered these women "right" or "wrong," meaningless to dwell upon the obvious, upon the coarsening of moral imagination to which such social idealism so often leads. To believe in "the greater good" is to operate, necessarily, in a certain ethical suspension. Ask anyone committed to Marxist analysis how many angels on the head of a pin, and you will be asked in return to never mind the angels, tell me who controls the production of pins.

To those of us who remain committed mainly to the exploration of moral distinctions and ambiguities, the feminist analysis may have seemed a particularly narrow and cracked determinism. Nonetheless it was serious, and for these high-strung idealists to find themselves out of the mimeo room and onto the Cavett show must have been in certain ways more unsettling to them than it ever was to the viewers. They were being heard, and yet not really. Attention was finally being paid, and yet that attention was mired in the trivial. Even the brightest movement women found themselves engaged in sullen public colloquies about the inequities of dishwashing and the intolerable humiliations of being observed by construction workers on Sixth Avenue. (This grievance was not atypic in that discussion of it seemed always to take on unexplored Ms. Scarlett overtones, suggestions of fragile cultivated flowers being "spoken to," and therefore violated, by uppity proles.) They totted up the pans scoured, the towels picked off the bathroom floor, the loads of laundry done in a lifetime. Cooking a meal could only be "dogwork," and to claim any pleasure from it was evidence of craven acquiescence in one's own forced labor. Small children could only be odious mechanisms for the spilling and digesting of food, for robbing women of their "freedom." It was a long way from Simone de Beauvoir's grave and awesome recognition of woman's role as "the Other" to the notion that the first step in changing that role was Alix Kates Shulman's marriage contract ("wife strips beds, husband remakes them"), a document reproduced in *Ms.*, but it was toward just such trivialization that the women's movement seemed to be heading.

Of course this litany of trivia was crucial to the

movement in the beginning, a key technique in the politicizing of women who had perhaps been conditioned to obscure their resentments even from themselves. Mrs. Shulman's discovery that she had less time than her husband seemed to have was precisely the kind of chord the movement had hoped to strike in all women (the "click! of recognition," as Jane O'Reilly described it), but such discoveries could be of no use at all if one refused to perceive the larger point, failed to make that inductive leap from the personal to the political. Splitting up the week into hours during which the children were directed to address their "personal questions" to either one parent or another might or might not have improved the quality of Mr. and Mrs. Shulman's marriage, but the improvement of marriages would not a revolution make. It could be very useful to call housework, as Lenin did, "the most unproductive, the most barbarous and the most arduous work a woman can do," but it could be useful only as the first step in a political process, only in the "awakening" of a class to its position, useful only as a metaphor: to believe, during the late Sixties and early Seventies in the United States of America, that the words had literal meaning was not only to stall the movement in the personal but to seriously delude oneself.

More and more, as the literature of the movement began to reflect the thinking of women who did not really understand the movement's ideological base, one had the sense of this stall, this delusion, the sense that the drilling of the theorists had struck only some psychic hardpan dense with superstitions and little sophistries, wish fulfillment, self-loathing and bitter fancies. To read even desultorily in this literature was to recognize instantly a certain dolorous phantasm, an imagined Everywoman with whom the authors seemed to identify all too entirely. This ubiquitous construct was everyone's victim but her own. She was persecuted even by her gynecologist, who made her beg in vain for contraceptives. She particularly needed contraceptives because she was raped on every date, raped by her husband, and raped finally on the abortionist's table. During the fashion for shoes with pointed toes, she, like "many women," had her toes amputated. She was so intimidated by cosmetics advertising that she would sleep "huge portions" of her day in order to forestall wrinkling, and when awake she was enslaved by detergent commercials on television. She sent her child to a nursery school where the little girls huddled in a "doll corner," and were forcibly restrained from playing with building blocks. Should she work she was paid "three to ten times less" than an (always) unqualified man holding the same job, was prevented from attending business lunches because she would be "embarrassed" to appear in public with a man not her husband, and, when she traveled alone, faced a choice between humiliation in a restaurant and "eating a doughnut" in her hotel room.

The half-truths, repeated, authenticated themselves. The bitter fancies assumed their own logic. To ask the obvious—why she did not get herself another gynecologist, another job, why she did not get out of bed and turn off the television set, or why, the most eccentric detail, she stayed in hotels where only doughnuts could be obtained from room service—was to join this argument at its own spooky level, a level which had only the most tenuous and unfortunate relationship to the actual condition of being a woman. That many women are victims of condescension and exploitation and sex-role stereotyping was scarcely news, but neither was it news that other women are not: nobody forces women to buy the package.

But of course something other than an objection to being "discriminated against" was at work here, something other than an aversion to being "stereotyped" in one's sex role. Increasingly it seemed that the aversion was to adult sexual life itself: how much cleaner to stay forever children. One is constantly struck, in the accounts of lesbian relationships which appear from time to time in movement literature, by the emphasis on the superior "tenderness" of the relationship, the "gentleness" of the sexual connection, as if the participants were wounded birds. The derogation of assertiveness as "machismo" has achieved such currency that one imagines several million women too delicate to deal at any level with an overtly heterosexual man. Just as one had gotten the unintended but inescapable suggestion, when told about the "terror and revulsion" experienced by women in the vicinity of construction sites, of creatures too "tender" for the abrasiveness of daily life, too fragile for the streets, so now one was getting, in the later literature of the movement, the impression of women too "sensitive" for the difficulties of adult life, women unequipped for reality and grasping at the movement as a rationale for denying that reality. The transient stab of dread and loss which accompanies menstruation simply never happens: we only thought it happened, because a male-chauvinist psychiatrist told us so. No woman need have bad dreams after an abortion: she has only been told she should. The power of sex is just an oppressive myth, no longer to be feared, because what the sexual connection really amounts to, we learn in one woman's account of a postmarital affair presented as liberated and liberating, is "wisecracking and laughing" and "lying together and then leaping up to play and sing the entire *Sesame Street Songbook.*" All one's actual apprehension of what it is like to be a woman, the irreconcilable difference of it—that sense of living one's deepest life underwater, that dark involvement with blood and birth and death—could now be declared invalid, unnecessary, *one never felt it at all.*

One was only told it, and now one is to be reprogrammed, fixed up, rendered again as inviolate and unstained as the "modern" little girls in the Tampax advertisements. More and more we have been hearing the wishful voices of just such perpetual adolescents, the voices of women scarred not by their class position as women but by the failure of their childhood expectations and misapprehensions. "Nobody ever so much as mentioned" to Susan Edmiston "that when you say 'I do,' what you are doing is not, as you thought, vowing your eternal love, but rather subscribing to a whole system of rights, obligations and responsibilities that may well be anathema to your most cherished beliefs." To Ellen Peck "the birth of children too often means the dissolution of romance, the loss of freedom, the abandonment of ideals to economics." A young woman described on the cover of *New York* as "The Suburban Housewife Who Bought the Promises of Women's Lib and Came to the City to Live Them" tells us what promises she bought: "The chance to respond to the bright lights and civilization of the Big Apple, yes. The chance to compete, yes. But most of all, the chance to have some fun. Fun is what's been missing."

Eternal love, romance, fun. The Big Apple. These are relatively rare expectations in the arrangements of consenting adults, although not in those of children, and it wrenches the heart to read about these women in their brave new lives. An ex-wife and mother of three speaks of her plan to "play out my college girl's dream. I am going to New York to become this famous writer. Or this working writer. Failing that, I will get a job in publishing." She mentions a friend, another young woman who "had never had any other life than as a daughter or wife or mother" but who is "just discovering herself to be a gifted potter." The childlike resourcefulness—to get a job in publishing, to become a gifted potter!—bewilders the imagination. The astral discontent with actual lives, actual men, the denial of the real generative possibilities of adult sexual life, somehow touches beyond words. "It is the right of the oppressed to organize around their oppression *as they see and define it,*" the movement theorists insist doggedly in an effort to solve the question of these women, to convince themselves that what is going on is still a political process, but the handwriting is already on the wall. These are converts who want not a revolution but "romance," who believe not in the oppression of women but in their own chances for a new life in exactly the mold of their old life. In certain ways they tell us sadder things about what the culture has done to them than the theorists ever did, and they also tell us, I suspect, that the movement is no longer a cause but a symptom.

1972

Doris Lessing

To read a great deal of Doris Lessing over a short span of time is to feel that the original hound of heaven has commandeered the attic. She holds the mind's other guests in ardent contempt. She appears for meals only to dismiss as decadent the household's own preoccupations with writing well. For more than twenty years now she has been registering, in a torrent of fiction that increasingly seems conceived in a stubborn rage against the very idea of fiction, every tremor along her emotional fault system, every slippage in her self-education. *Look here,* she is forever demanding, a missionary devoid of any but the most didactic irony: *The Communist Party is not the answer. There is a life beyond vaginal orgasm. St. John of the Cross was not as dotty as certain Anglicans would have had you believe.* She comes hard to ideas, and, once she has collared one, worries it with Victorian doggedness.

That she is a writer of considerable native power, a "natural" writer in the Dreiserian mold, someone who can close her eyes and "give" a situation by the sheer force of her emotional energy, seems almost a stain on her conscience. She views her real gift for fiction much as she views her own biology, as another trick to entrap her. She does not want to "write well." Her leaden disregard for even the simplest rhythms of language, her arrogantly bad ear for dialogue—all of that is beside her own point. More and more, Mrs. Lessing writes exclusively in the service of immediate cosmic reform: she wants to write, as the writer Anna in *The Golden Notebook* wanted to write, only to "create a new way of looking at life."

Consider *Briefing for a Descent into Hell.* Here Mrs. Lessing gave us a novel exclusively of "ideas," not a novel about the play of ideas in the lives of certain characters but a novel in which the characters exist only as markers in the presentation of an idea. The situation in the novel was this: a well-dressed but disheveled man is found wandering, an amnesiac, on the embankment near the Waterloo Bridge in London. He is taken by the police to a psychiatric hospital where, in the face of total indifference on his part, attempts are made to identify him. He is Charles Watkins, a professor of classics at Cambridge. An authority in his field, an occasional lecturer on more general topics. Lately a stammerer. Lately prone to bad evenings during which he condemns not only his own but all academic disciplines as "pigswill." A fifty-year-old man who finally cracked, and in cracking personified Mrs. Lessing's conviction that "the millions who have cracked" were "making cracks where the light could shine through at last." For of course the "nonsense" that Charles Watkins talks in the hospital makes, to the reader although not to the doctors, unmistakable "sense."

So pronounced was Charles Watkins' acumen about the inner reality of those around him that much of the time *Briefing for a Descent into Hell* read like a selective case study from an R. D. Laing book. The reality Charles Watkins describes is familiar to anyone who has ever had a high fever, or been exhausted to the point of breaking, or is just on the whole only marginally engaged in the dailiness of life. He experiences the loss of ego, the apprehension of the cellular nature of all matter, the "oneness" of things that seems always to lie just past the edge of controlled conscious thought. He hallucinates, or "remembers," the nature of the universe. He "remembers"—or is on the verge of remembering, before electroshock obliterates the memory and returns him to "sanity"—something very like a "briefing" for life on earth.

The details of this briefing were filled in by Mrs. Lessing, only too relieved to abandon the strain of creating character and slip into her own rather more exhortative voice. Imagine an interplanetary conference, convened on Venus to discuss once again the problem of the self-destructive planet Earth. (The fancy that extraterrestrial life is by definition of a higher order than our own is one that soothes all children, and many writers.) The procedure is this: certain superior beings descend to Earth brainprinted with the task of arousing the planet to its folly. These emissaries have, once on Earth, no memory of their more enlightened life. They wake slowly to their mission. They recognize one another only vaguely, and do not remember why. We are to understand, of course, that Charles Watkins is among those who have made the Descent, whether literal or metaphorical, and is now, for just so long as he can resist therapy, awake. This is the initial revelation in the book, and it is also the only one.

Even given Mrs. Lessing's tendency to confront all ideas *tabula rasa,* we are dealing here with less than astonishing stuff. The idea that there is sanity in insanity, that truth lies on the far side of madness, informs not only a considerable spread of Western literature but also, so commonly is it now held, an entire generation's experiment with hallucinogens. Most of Mrs. Lessing's thoughts about the cultural definition of insanity reflect or run parallel to those of Laing, and yet the idea was already so prevalent that Laing cannot even be said to have popularized it: his innovation was only to have taken it out of the realm of instinctive knowledge and into the limited context of psychiatric therapy. Although Mrs. Lessing apparently thought the content of *Briefing for a Descent into Hell* so startling that she was impelled to add an explanatory afterword, a two-page parable about the ignorance of certain psychiatrists at large London teaching hospitals, she had herself dealt before with this very material. In *The Golden Notebook* Anna makes this note for a story: "A man whose 'sense of reality' has gone; and because of it, has a deeper sense of reality than 'normal' people." By the time Mrs. Lessing finished *The Four-Gated City* she had refined the proposition: Lynda Coldridge's deeper sense of reality is not the result but the definition of her madness. So laboriously is this notion developed in the closing three hundred pages of *The Four-Gated City* that one would have thought that Mrs. Lessing had more or less exhausted its literary possibilities.

But she was less and less interested in literary possibilities, which is where we strike the faultline. "If I saw it in terms of an artistic problem, then it'd be easy, wouldn't it," Anna tells her friend Molly, in *The Golden Notebook,* as explanation of her disinclination to write another book. "We could have ever such intelligent chats about the modern novel." This may seem a little on the easy side, even to the reader who is willing to overlook Anna's later assertion that she cannot write because "a Chinese peasant" is looking over her shoulder. ("Or one of Castro's guerrilla fighters. Or an Algerian fighting in the F.L.N.") *Madame Bovary* told us more about bourgeois life than several generations of Marxists have, but there does not seem much doubt that Flaubert saw it as an artistic problem.

That Mrs. Lessing does not suggests her particular dilemma. What we are witnessing here is a writer undergoing a profound and continuing cultural trauma, a woman of determinedly utopian and distinctly teleological bent assaulted at every turn by fresh evidence that the world is not exactly improving as promised. And, because such is the particular quality of her mind, she is compelled in the face of this evidence to look even more frenetically for the final cause, the unambiguous answer.

In the beginning her search was less frenzied. She came out of Southern Rhodesia imprinted ineradicably by precisely the kind of rigid agrarian world that most easily makes storytellers of its exiled children. What British Africa gave her, besides those images of a sky so empty and a society so inflexible as to make the slightest tremor in either worth remarking upon, was a way of perceiving the rest of her life: for a long time to come she could interpret all she saw in terms of "injustice," not merely the injustice of white man to black, of colonizer to colonized, but the more general injustices of class and particularly of sex. She grew up knowing not only what hard frontiers do to women but what women then do to the men who keep them there. She could hear in all her memories that "voice of the suffering female" passed on from mothers to daughters in a chain broken only at great cost.

Of these memories she wrote a first novel, *The Grass Is Singing,* entirely traditional in its conventions. Reality was *there,* waiting to be observed by an omniscient third person. *The Grass Is Singing* was neat in its construction, relatively scrupulous in its maintenance of tone, predicated upon a world of constants. Its characters moved through that world unconscious of knowledge shared by author and reader. The novel was, in brief, everything Mrs. Lessing was to reject as "false" and "evasive" by the time she wrote *The Golden Notebook*. "Why not write down, simply, what happened between Molly and her son today?" Anna demands of herself. "Why do I never write down, simply, what happens? Why don't I keep a diary? Obviously, my changing everything into fiction is simply a means of concealing something from myself. . . . I shall keep a diary."

It would be hard to imagine a character more unrelievedly self-conscious, or more insistently the author's surrogate, than Anna Gould in *The Golden Notebook*. The entire intention of the novel is to shatter the conventional distance of fiction, to deny all distinction between toad and garden, to "write down, simply, what happens." Call the writer Anna Gould or call her Doris Lessing, *The Golden Notebook* is the diary of a writer in shock. There she is in London, 1950. A young woman determined to forge a life as a "free woman," as an "intellectual," she has come out of a simple society into what Robert Penn Warren once called the convulsion of the world, and she is finding some equivocation in the answers so clear to her in Africa. Her expectations give off a bright and dated valiance. Her disenchantments are all too familiar. The sheer will, the granitic ambitiousness of *The Golden Notebook* overrides everything else about it. Great raw hunks of undigested experience, unedited transcripts of what happened between Molly and her son today, overwhelming memories and rejections of those memories as sentimental, the fracturing of a sensibility beginning for the first time to doubt its perceptions: all of it runs out of the teller's mind and into the reader's with deliberate disregard for the nature of the words in between. The teller creates "characters" and "scenes" only to deny their validity. She berates herself for clinging to the "certainty" of her memories in the face of the general uncertainty. Mrs. Lessing looms through *The Golden Notebook* as a woman driven by doubts not only about what to tell but about the validity of telling it at all.

Yet she continued to write, and to write fiction. Not until the end of the five-volume *Children of Violence* series did one sense a weakening of that compulsion to remember, and a metastasis of that cognitive frenzy for answers. She had seen, by then, a great deal go, had seized a great many answers and lost them. Organized politics went early. Freudian determinism seemed incompatible. The Africa of her memory was another country. The voice she felt most deeply, that of women trying to define their relationships to one another and to men, first went shrill and then, appropriated by and reduced to a "movement," slipped below the range of her attention. She had been betrayed by all those answers and more, and yet, increasingly possessed, her only response has been to look for another. That she is scarcely alone in this possession is what lends her quest its great interest: the impulse to final solutions has been not only Mrs. Lessing's dilemma but the guiding delusion of her time. It is not an impulse I hold high, but there is something finally very moving about her tenacity.

1971

Georgia O'Keeffe

"WHERE I WAS BORN and where and how I have lived is unimportant," Georgia O'Keeffe told us in the book of paintings and words published in her ninetieth year on earth. She seemed to be advising us to forget the beautiful face in the Stieglitz photographs. She appeared to be dismissing the rather condescending romance that had attached to her by then, the romance of extreme good looks and advanced age and deliberate isolation. "It is what I have done with where I have been that should be of interest." I recall an August afternoon in Chicago in 1973 when I took my daughter, then seven, to see what Georgia O'Keeffe had done with where she had been. One of the vast O'Keeffe "Sky Above Clouds" canvases floated over the back stairs in the Chicago Art Institute that day, dominating what seemed to be several stories of empty light, and my daughter looked at it once, ran to the landing, and kept on looking. "Who drew it," she whispered after a while. I told her. "I need to talk to her," she said finally.

My daughter was making, that day in Chicago, an entirely unconscious but quite basic assumption about people and the work they do. She was assuming that the glory she saw in the work reflected a glory in its maker, that the painting was the painter as the poem is the poet, that every choice one made alone—every word chosen or rejected, every brush stroke laid or not laid down—betrayed one's character. *Style is character.* It seemed to me that afternoon that I had rarely seen so instinctive an application of this familiar principle, and I recall being pleased not only that my daughter responded to style as character but that it was Georgia O'Keeffe's particular style to which she responded: this was a hard woman who had imposed her 192 square feet of clouds on Chicago.

"Hardness" has not been in our century a quality much admired in women, nor in the past twenty years has it even been in official favor for men. When hardness surfaces in the very old we tend to transform it into "crustiness" or eccentricity, some tonic pepperiness to be indulged at a distance. On the evidence of her work and what she has said about it, Georgia O'Keeffe is neither "crusty" nor eccentric. She is simply hard, a straight shooter, a woman clean of received wisdom and open to what she sees. This is a woman who could early on dismiss most of her contemporaries as "dreamy," and would later single out one she liked as "a very poor painter." (And then add, apparently by way of softening the judgment: "I guess he wasn't a painter at all. He had no courage and I believe that to create one's own world in any of the arts takes courage.") This is a woman who in 1939 could advise her admirers that they were missing her point, that their appreciation of her famous flowers was merely sentimental. "When I paint a red hill," she observed coolly in the catalogue for an exhibition that year, "you say it is too bad that I don't always paint flowers. A flower touches almost everyone's heart. A red hill doesn't touch everyone's heart." This is a woman who could describe the genesis of one of her most well-known paintings—the "Cow's Skull: Red, White and Blue" owned by the Metropolitan—as an act of quite deliberate and derisive orneriness. "I thought of the city men I had been seeing in the East," she wrote. "They talked so often of writing the Great American Novel—the Great American Play—the Great American Poetry. . . . So as I was painting my cow's head on blue I thought to myself, 'I'll make it an American painting. They will not think it great with the red stripes down the sides—Red, White and Blue—but they will notice it.' "

The city men. The men. They. The words crop up again and again as this astonishingly aggressive woman tells us what was on her mind when she was making her astonishingly aggressive paintings. It was those city men who stood accused of sentimentalizing her flowers: "I made you take time to look at what I saw and when you took time to really notice my flower you hung all your associations with flowers on my flower and you write about my flower as if I think and see what you think and see—and I don't." *And I don't.* Imagine those words spoken, and the sound you hear is *don't tread on me.* "The men" believed it impossible to paint New York, so Georgia O'Keeffe painted New York. "The men" didn't think much of her bright color, so she made it brighter. The men yearned toward Europe so she went to Texas, and then New Mexico. The men talked about Cézanne, "long involved remarks about the 'plastic quality' of his form and color," and took one another's long involved remarks, in the view of this angelic rattlesnake in their midst, altogether too seriously. "I can paint one of those dismal-colored paintings like the men," the woman who regarded herself always as an outsider remembers thinking one day in 1922, and she did: a painting of a shed "all low-toned and dreary with the tree beside the door." She called this act of rancor "The Shanty" and hung it in her next show. "The men seemed to approve of it," she reported fifty-four years later, her contempt undimmed. "They seemed to think that maybe I was beginning to paint. That was my only low-toned dismal-colored painting."

Some women fight and others do not. Like so many successful guerrillas in the war between the sexes, Georgia O'Keeffe seems to have been equipped early with an immutable sense of who she was and a fairly clear understanding that she would be required to prove it. On the surface her upbringing was conventional. She was a child on the Wisconsin prairie who played with china dolls and painted watercolors with cloudy skies because sunlight was too hard to paint and, with her brother and sisters, listened every night to her mother read stories of the Wild West, of Texas, of Kit Carson and Billy the Kid. She told adults that she wanted to be an artist and was embarrassed when they asked what kind of artist she wanted to be: she had no idea "what kind." She had no idea what artists did. She had never seen a picture that interested her, other than a pen-and-ink Maid of Athens in one of her mother's books, some Mother Goose illustrations printed on cloth, a tablet cover that showed a little girl with pink roses, and the painting of Arabs on horseback that hung in her grandmother's parlor. At thirteen, in a Dominican convent, she was mortified when the sister corrected her drawing. At Chatham Episcopal Institute in Virginia she painted lilacs and sneaked time alone to walk out to where she could see the line of the Blue Ridge Mountains on the horizon. At the Art Institute in Chicago she was shocked by the presence of live models and wanted to abandon anatomy lessons. At the Art Students League in New York one of her fellow students advised her that, since he would be a great painter and she would end up teaching painting in a girls' school, any work of hers was less important than modeling for him. Another painted over her work to show her how the Impressionists did trees. She had not before heard how the Impressionists did trees and she did not much care.

At twenty-four she left all those opinions behind and went for the first time to live in Texas, where there were no trees to paint and no one to tell her how not to paint them. In Texas there was only the horizon she craved. In Texas she had her sister Claudia with her for a while, and in the late afternoons they would walk away from town and toward the horizon and watch the evening star come out. "That evening star fascinated me," she wrote. "It was in some way very exciting to me. My sister had a gun, and as we walked she would throw bottles into the air and shoot as many as she could before they hit the ground. I had nothing but to walk into nowhere and the wide sunset space with the star. Ten watercolors were made from that star." In a way one's interest is compelled as much by the sister Claudia with the gun as by the painter Georgia with the star, but only the painter left us this shining record. Ten watercolors were made from that star.

1976

IV /

SOJOURNS

In the Islands

1969: I had better tell you where I am, and why. I am sitting in a high-ceilinged room in the Royal Hawaiian Hotel in Honolulu watching the long translucent curtains billow in the trade wind and trying to put my life back together. My husband is here, and our daughter, age three. She is blond and barefoot, a child of paradise in a frangipani lei, and she does not understand why she cannot go to the beach. She cannot go to the beach because there has been an earthquake in the Aleutians, 7.5 on the Richter scale, and a tidal wave is expected. In two or three minutes the wave, if there is one, will hit Midway Island, and we are awaiting word from Midway. My husband watches the television screen. I watch the curtains, and imagine the swell of the water.

The bulletin, when it comes, is a distinct anticlimax: Midway reports no unusual wave action. My husband switches off the television set and stares out the window. I avoid his eyes, and brush the baby's hair. In the absence of a natural disaster we are left again to our own uneasy devices. We are here on this island in the middle of the Pacific in lieu of filing for divorce.

I tell you this not as aimless revelation but because I want you to know, as you read me, precisely who I am and where I am and what is on my mind. I want you to understand exactly what you are getting:

you are getting a woman who for some time now has felt radically separated from most of the ideas that seem to interest other people. You are getting a woman who somewhere along the line misplaced whatever slight faith she ever had in the social contract, in the meliorative principle, in the whole grand pattern of human endeavor. Quite often during the past several years I have felt myself a sleepwalker, moving through the world unconscious of the moment's high issues, oblivious to its data, alert only to the stuff of bad dreams, the children burning in the locked car in the supermarket parking lot, the bike boys stripping down stolen cars on the captive cripple's ranch, the freeway sniper who feels "real bad" about picking off the family of five, the hustlers, the insane, the cunning Okie faces that turn up in military investigations, the sullen lurkers in doorways, the lost children, all the ignorant armies jostling in the night. Acquaintances read *The New York Times*, and try to tell me the news of the world. I listen to call-in shows.

You will perceive that such a view of the world presents difficulties. I have trouble making certain connections. I have trouble maintaining the basic notion that keeping promises matters in a world where everything I was taught seems beside the point. The point itself seems increasingly obscure. I came into adult life equipped with an essentially romantic ethic, holding always before me the examples of Axel Heyst in *Victory* and Milly Theale in *The Wings of the Dove* and Charlotte Rittenmayer in *The Wild Palms* and a few dozen others like them, believing as they did that salvation lay in extreme and doomed commitments, promises made and somehow kept outside the range of normal social experience. I still believe that, but I have trouble reconciling salvation with those ignorant armies camped in my mind. I could indulge here in a little idle generalization, could lay off my own state of profound emotional shock on the larger cultural breakdown, could talk fast about convulsions in the society and alienation and anomie and maybe even assassination, but that would be just one more stylish shell game. I am not the society in microcosm. I am a thirty-four-year-old woman with long straight hair and an old bikini bathing suit and bad nerves sitting on an island in the middle of the Pacific waiting for a tidal wave that will not come.

We spend, my husband and I and the baby, a restorative week in paradise. We are each the other's model of consideration, tact, restraint at the very edge of the precipice. He refrains from noticing when I am staring at nothing, and in turn I refrain from dwelling at length upon a newspaper story about a couple who apparently threw their infant and then themselves into the boiling crater of a live volcano on Maui. We also refrain from mentioning any kicked-down doors, hospitalized psychotics, any chronic anxieties or packed suitcases. We lie in the sun, drive out through the cane to Waimea Bay. We breakfast on the terrace, and gray-haired women smile benevolently at us. I smile back. Happy families are all alike on the terrace of the Royal Hawaiian Hotel in Honolulu. My husband comes in from Kalakaua Avenue one morning and tells me that he has seen a six-foot-two drag queen we know in Los Angeles. Our acquaintance was shopping, my husband reports, for a fishnet bikini and did not speak. We both laugh. I am reminded that we laugh at the same things, and read him this complaint from a very old copy of *Honolulu* magazine I picked up in someone's office:

"When President Johnson recently came to Honolulu, the morning paper's banner read something like 'PICKETS TO GREET PRESIDENT.' Would it not have been just as newsworthy to say 'WARM ALOHA TO GREET PRESIDENT'?" At the end of the week I tell my husband that I am going to try harder to make things matter. My husband says that he has heard that before, but the air is warm and the baby has another frangipani lei and there is no rancor in his voice. Maybe it can be all right, I say. Maybe, he says.

1970: Quite early every morning in Honolulu, on that stretch of Waikiki Beach which fronts the Royal Hawaiian Hotel, an employee of the hotel spends fifteen or twenty minutes raking the sand within a roped enclosure reserved for registered guests. Since this "private" beach differs from the "public" beach only by its raked sand, its rope, and its further remove from the water, it is at first difficult to see why anyone would sit there, but people do. They sit there all day long and in great numbers, facing the sea in even rows.

I had been an occasional visitor to Honolulu for several years before I entirely perceived that the roped beach was central to the essence of the Royal Hawaiian, that the point of sitting there was not at all exclusivity, as is commonly supposed on Waikiki, but inclusivity. Anyone behind the rope is presumed to be, by tacit definition, "our kind." Anyone behind the rope will watch over our children as we will watch over theirs, will not palm room keys or smoke dope or listen to Creedence Clearwater on a transistor when we are awaiting word from the Mainland on the prime rate.

Anyone behind the rope, should we venture conversation, will "know people we know": the Royal's roped beach is an enclave of apparent strangers ever on the verge of discovering that their nieces roomed in Lagunita at Stanford the same year, or that their best friends lunched together during the last Crosby. The fact that anyone behind the rope would understand the word "Crosby" to signify a golf tournament at Pebble Beach suggests the extent to which the Royal Hawaiian is not merely a hotel but a social idea, one of the few extant clues to a certain kind of American life.

Of course great hotels have always been social ideas, flawless mirrors to the particular societies they service. Had there never been an Empire there would not have been a Raffles. To understand what the Royal is now you must first understand what it was, from 1927 through the Thirties, the distant and mildly exotic "pink palace" of the Pacific, the resort built by the Matson Line to rival and surpass such hotels as the Coronado, the Broadmoor, Del Monte. Standing then almost alone on Waikiki, the Royal made Honolulu a place to go, made all things "Hawaiian"—leis, ukuleles, luaus, coconut-leaf hats and the singing of "I Wanna Learn to Speak Hawaiian"—a decade's craze at country-club dances across the United States. During the fourteen years between the Royal's opening and Pearl Harbor people came in on the Matson Line's *Malolo* and *Lurline* and they brought with them not only steamer trunks but children and grandchildren and valets and nurses and silver Rolls-Royces and ultramarine-blue Packard roadsters. They "wintered" at the Royal, or "summered" there, or "spent several months." They came to the Royal to rest "after hunting in South Africa." They went home "by way of Banff and Lake Louise." In Honolulu there was polo, golf, bowling on the green. Every afternoon the Royal served tea on rattan tables. The maids wove leis for every guest. The chefs constructed, as table decoration, the United States Capitol Building in Hawaiian sugar.

The Royal's scrapbooks for those years survive as an index to America's industrial fortunes, large and small. Mellons and Du Ponts and Gettys and the man who had just patented the world's largest incubator (47,000-egg capacity) seem to differ not at all from one another, photographed at the Royal in 1928. Dorothy Spreckels strums a ukulele on the verandah. Walter P. Chrysler, Jr., arrives with his mother and father for a season at the Royal. A figure on the beach is described as "a Colorado Springs society woman," a young couple as "prominently identified with the young-married set in Akron." At the Royal they met not only one another but a larger world as well: Australian station owners, Ceylonese tea planters, Cuban sugar operators.

In the faded photographs one sees mostly mothers and daughters. The men, when they are present, display in the main an affecting awkwardness, an awareness that they have harsher roles, say as mayor of Seattle or president of the Overland Motor Company, a resistance to the world of summering and wintering. In 1931 the son of President Hoover spent time at the Royal, was widely entertained, caught thirty-eight fish off the Kona coast of Hawaii, and had his picture taken on the Royal beach shaking hands with Duke Kahanamoku. This photograph appeared in *Town and Country*, which also reported in 1931 that "the diving boys in Honolulu harbor say that fishing has been good and there are no indications of hard times in the denominations of coins flipped to them as bait from incoming steamers."

Nor did the turnings of the Sixties effect much change at the Royal. What the place reflected in the Thirties it reflects still, in less flamboyant mutations: a kind of life lived always on the streets where the oldest trees grow. It is a life so secure in its traditional concerns that the cataclysms of the larger society disturb it only as surface storms disturb the sea's bottom, a long time later and in oblique ways. It is a life lived by millions of people in this country and largely forgotten by most of us. Sometimes I think I remember it only at the Royal Hawaiian. There in the warm early evenings, the women in turquoise-blue and buttercup-yellow chiffons seem, as they wait for cars under the pink porte-cochere, the natural inheritors of a style later seized upon by Patricia Nixon and her daughters. In the mornings, when the beach is just raked and the air damp and sweet from the dawn rain, I see the same women, now in printed silks and lined cashmere cardigans, eating papaya on the terrace just as they have done every few seasons since they were young girls, in the late Twenties, and came to the Royal with their mothers and sisters. Their husbands scan the San Francisco and Los Angeles papers with the practiced disinterest of men who believe their lives safe in municipal bonds. These papers arrive at the Royal one and sometimes two days late, which lends the events of the day a peculiar and unsettling distance. I recall overhearing a conversation at the Royal's newsstand on the morning after the California primary in June 1968, the morning Robert Kennedy lay dying in Good Samaritan Hospital in Los Angeles. "How'd the primary go?" a man buying cigarettes asked his wife. She studied the day-old headlines. " 'Early Turnout Heavy,' " she said. Later in the morning I overheard this woman discussing the assassination: her husband had heard the news when he dropped by a brokerage office to get the day's New York closings.

To sit by the Royal pool and read *The New York Review of Books* is to feel oneself an asp, disguised in a voile beach robe, in the very bosom of the place. I put *The New York Review of Books* aside and talk to a pretty young woman who has honeymooned at the Royal, because honeymoons at the Royal are a custom in her family, with each of her three husbands. My daughter makes friends at the pool with another four-year-old, Jill, from Fairbanks, Alaska, and it is taken for granted by Jill's mother and aunt that the two children will meet again, year after year, in the immutable pleasant rhythms of a life that used to be, and at the Royal Hawaiian seems still to be. I sit in my voile beach robe and watch the children and wish, against all the evidence I know, that it might be so.

1970: To look down upon Honolulu from the high rain forest that divides windward Oahu from the leeward city is to see, in the center of an extinct volcano named Puowaina, a place so still and private that once seen it is forever in the mind. There are banyan trees in the crater, and rain trees, and 19,500 graves. Yellow primavera blazes on the hills above. Whole slopes seem clouded in mauve jacaranda. This is the place commonly called Punchbowl, the National Memorial Cemetery of the Pacific, and 13,000 of the dead in its crater were killed during World War II. Some of the rest died in Korea. For almost a decade now, in the outer sections just inside the rim of the crater, they have been digging graves for Americans killed in Vietnam, not many, a fraction of the total, one, two, three a week, most of them Island boys but some of them carried here by families who live thousands of miles across the Pacific, a gesture that touches by its very difficulty. Because the Vietnam dead are shipped first to Travis A.F.B. in California and then to the next of kin, those Mainland families burying their sons or husbands in Honolulu must bring the bodies back over the Pacific one last time. The superintendent of Punchbowl, Martin T. Corley, refers to such burials as his "ship-in Vietnams."

"A father or an uncle calls me from the Mainland and he says they're bringing their boy here, I don't ask why," Mr. Corley said when I talked to him not long ago. We were sitting in his office in the crater and on the wall hung the Bronze Star and Silver Star citations he had received in Europe in 1944, Martin T. Corley, a man in an aloha shirt who had gone from South Ozone Park in Queens to the Battle of the Bulge to a course in cemetery management at Fort Sam Houston and finally, twenty-some years later, to an office in an extinct volcano in the Pacific from which he could watch the quick and the dead in still another war.

I watched him leafing through a stack of what he called "transmittals," death forms from Vietnam. There in Martin T. Corley's office Vietnam seemed considerably less chimerical than it had seemed on the Mainland for some months, less last year's war, less successfully consigned to that limbo of benign neglect in which any mention of continuing casualties was made to seem a little counterproductive, a little démodé. There in the crater it seemed less easy to believe that weekly killed-in-action figures under 100 might by some sleight-of-hand add up to zero, a nonexistent war. There in sight of the automatic gravediggers what the figures added up to, for the first twelve weeks of 1970, was 1,078 dead. Martin T. Corley gets a transmittal on each of them. He holds these transmittal forms for fifteen or twenty days before throwing them away, just in case a family wants to bring its dead to Punchbowl. "See, we had a family bring a boy in from Oregon a few days ago," he said. "We've got a California coming in now. We figure they've got their reasons. We pick the plot, open the grave. These ship-in families, we don't see them until the hearse comes through the gate."

On a warm windy afternoon a few days later I stood with Mr. Corley on the soft grass up in Section K of the crater and waited for one such family to come through the gate. They had flown out from the Mainland with the body the night before, six of them, the mother and father and a sister and her husband and a couple of other relatives, and they would bury their boy in the afternoon sun and fly back a few hours later. We waited, and we watched, and then, on the road below, the six Air Force pallbearers snapped to attention. The bugler jumped up from beneath a banyan tree and took his place behind the honor guard. We could see the hearse then, winding up and around the circular road to Section K, the hearse and two cars, their headlights dim in the tropical sun. "Two of us from the office come to all the Vietnams," Mr. Corley said suddenly. "I mean in case the family breaks down or something."

All I can tell you about the next ten minutes is that they seemed a very long time. We watched the coffin being carried to the grave and we watched the pallbearers lift the flag, trying to hold it taut in the warm trade wind. The wind was blowing hard, toppling the vases of gladioli set by the grave, obliterating some of the chaplain's words. "If God is for us then who can be against us," the chaplain said, a red-headed young major in suntans, and then I did not hear any more for a while. I was standing behind the six canvas chairs where the family sat, standing there with Mr. Corley and an Air Force survival assistance officer, and I was looking beyond the chaplain to a scattering of graves so fresh they had no headstones, just plastic markers stuck in the ground. "We tenderly commit this body to the ground," the chaplain said then. The men in the honor guard raised their rifles. Three shots cracked out. The bugler played taps. The pallbearers folded the flag until only the blue field and a few stars showed, and one of them stepped forward to present the flag to the father. For the first time the father looked away from the coffin, looked away from the pallbearers and out across the expanse of graves. A slight man with his face trembling and his eyes wet, he stood facing Mr. Corley and me, and for a moment we looked directly at each other, but he was seeing not me, not Mr. Corley, not anyone.

It was not quite three o'clock. The father, transferring the flag from hand to hand as if it burned, said a few halting words to the pallbearers. I walked away from the grave then, down to my car, and waited for Mr. Corley to talk to the father. He wanted to tell the father that if he and his wife wanted to come back before their plane left, the grave would be covered by four o'clock. "Sometimes it makes them feel better to see it," Mr. Corley said when he caught up with me. "Sometimes they get on the plane and they worry, you know, it didn't get covered." His voice trailed off. "We cover within thirty minutes," he said finally. "Fill, cover, get the marker on. That's one thing I remember from my training." We stood there a moment in the warm wind, then said goodbye. The pallbearers filed onto the Air Force bus. The bugler walked past, whistling "Raindrops Keep Fallin' on My Head." Just after four o'clock the father and mother came back and looked for a long while at the covered grave, then took a night flight back to the Mainland. Their son was one of 101 Americans killed that week in Vietnam.

1975: The 8:45 A.M. Pan American to Honolulu this morning was delayed half an hour before takeoff from Los Angeles. During this delay the stewardesses served orange juice and coffee and two children played tag in the aisles and, somewhere behind me, a man began screaming at a woman who seemed to be his wife. I say that the woman seemed to be his wife only because the tone of his invective sounded practiced, although the only words I heard clearly were these: "You are driving me to murder." After a moment I was aware of the door to the plane being opened a few rows behind me, and of the man rushing off. There were many Pan American employees rushing on and off then, and considerable confusion. I do not know whether the man reboarded the plane before takeoff or whether the woman came on to Honolulu alone, but I thought about it all the way across the Pacific. I thought about it while I was drinking a sherry-on-the-rocks and I thought about it during lunch and I was still thinking about it when the first of the Hawaiian Islands appeared off the left wing tip. It was not until we had passed Diamond Head and were coming in low over the reef for landing at Honolulu, however, that I realized what I most disliked about this incident: I disliked it because it had the aspect of a short story, one of those "little epiphany" stories in which the main character glimpses a crisis in a stranger's life—a woman weeping in a tearoom, often, or an accident seen from the window of a train, "tearooms" and "trains" still being fixtures of short stories although not of real life—and is moved to see his or her own life in a new light. I was not going to Honolulu because I wanted to see life reduced to a short story. I was going to Honolulu because I wanted to see life expanded to a novel, and I still do. I wanted room for flowers, and reef fish, and people who may or may not be driving one another to murder but in any case are not impelled, by the demands of narrative convention, to say so out loud on the 8:45 A.M. Pan American to Honolulu.

1977: I have never seen a postcard of Hawaii that featured Schofield Barracks. Schofield is off the track, off the tour, hard by the shadowy pools of the Wahiawa Reservoir, and to leave Honolulu and drive inland to Schofield is to sense a clouding of the atmosphere, a darkening of the color range. The translucent pastels of the famous coast give way to the opaque greens of interior Oahu. Crushed white coral gives way to red dirt, sugar dirt, deep red laterite soil that crumbles soft in the hand and films over grass and boots and hubcaps. Clouds mass over the Waianae Range. Cane fires smoke on the horizon and rain falls fitfully. BUY SOME COLLARD GREENS, reads a sign on a weathered frame grocery in Wahiawa, just across the two-lane bridge from the Schofield gate. MASSAGE PARLOR, CHECKS

CASHED, 50TH STATE POOLROOM, HAPPY HOUR, CASH FOR CARS. Schofield Loan. Schofield Pawn. Schofield Sands Motor Lodge. Then, finally, Schofield itself, the Schofield we all know from James Jones's *From Here to Eternity*, the Schofield that is Home of the 25th "Tropic Lightning" Infantry Division, formerly the Hawaii Division, James Jones's own division, Robert E. Lee Prewitt's division, Maggio's and Warden's and Stark's and Dynamite Holmes's division, *Fit to Fight, Trained to Win, Ready to Go. All Wars Are Won in the End by the Infantryman. Through These Portals Pass the Finest Soldiers in the World—25TH INFANTRY DIVISION SOLDIERS. TROPIC LIGHTNING REENLISTMENT.* I have never driven into Schofield and seen those words without hearing the blues that end *From Here to Eternity:*

Got paid out on Monday
Not a dog soldier no more
They gimme all that money
So much my pockets is sore
More dough than I can use. Reenlistment Blues.
Ain't no time to lose. Reenlistment Blues.

Certain places seem to exist mainly because someone has written about them. Kilimanjaro belongs to Ernest Hemingway. Oxford, Mississippi, belongs to William Faulkner, and one hot July week in Oxford I was moved to spend an afternoon walking the graveyard looking for his stone, a kind of courtesy call on the owner of the property. A place belongs forever to whoever claims it hardest, remembers it most obsessively, wrenches it from itself, shapes it, renders it, loves it so radically that he remakes it in his image, and not only Schofield Barracks but a great deal of Honolulu itself has always belonged for me to James Jones. The first time I ever saw Hotel Street in Honolulu was on a Saturday night in 1966 when all the bars and tattoo parlors were full of military police and girls looking for a dollar and nineteen-year-olds, on their way to or from Saigon, looking for a girl. I recall looking that night for the particular places that had figured in *From Here to Eternity:* the Black Cat, the Blue Anchor, the whorehouse Jones called the New Congress Hotel. I remember driving up Wilhemina Rise to look for Alma's house and I remember walking out of the Royal Hawaiian Hotel and expecting to see Prewitt and Maggio sitting on the curb and I remember walking the Waialae Country Club golf course, trying to figure exactly where Prewitt died. I think it was in the trap near the fifth green.

It is hard to see one of these places claimed by fiction without a sudden blurring, a slippage, a certain vertiginous occlusion of the imagined and the real, and this slippage was particularly acute the last time I arrived in Honolulu, on a June day when the author of *From Here to Eternity* had been dead just a few weeks. In New York the death of James Jones had been the occasion for many considerations and reconsiderations. Many mean guilts had been recalled and exorcised. Many lessons had been divined, in both the death and the life. In Honolulu the death of James Jones had been marked by the publication, in the *Honolulu Star-Bulletin,* of an excerpt from the author's *Viet Journal,* the epilogue, the part in which he talked about returning to Honolulu in 1973 and looking for the places he had remembered in *From Here to Eternity* but had last seen in 1942, when he was twenty-one years old and shipped out for Guadalcanal with the 25th Division. In

1973 the five pillboxes on Makapuu Head had seemed to James Jones exactly as he had left them in 1942. In 1973 the Royal Hawaiian Hotel had seemed to James Jones less formidably rich than he had left it in 1942, and it had occurred to him with considerable poignance that he was a man in his fifties who could walk into the Royal Hawaiian and buy whatever he wanted.

He had bought a beer and gone back to Paris. In June of 1977 he was dead and it was not possible to buy a copy of his great novel, his living novel, the novel in which he so loved Honolulu that he remade it in his image, in any of Honolulu's largest bookstores. "Is it a best-seller?" I was asked in one, and the golden child in charge of another suggested that I try the psychic-science shelf. In that instant I thought I grieved for James Jones, a man I never met, but I think I grieved for all of us: for Jones, for myself, for the sufferers of mean guilts and for their exorcists, for Robert E. Lee Prewitt, for the Royal Hawaiian Hotel and for this golden nitwit who believed eternity to be a psychic science.

I have never been sure whether the extreme gravity of *From Here to Eternity* is an exact reflection of the light at Schofield Barracks or whether I see the light as grave because I have read James Jones. "It had rained all morning and then suddenly cleared at noon, and the air, freshly washed today, was like dark crystal in the sharp clarity and sombre focus it gave to every image." It was in this sombre focus that James Jones rendered Schofield, and it was in this sombre focus that I last saw Schofield, one Monday during that June. It had rained in the morning and the smell of eucalyptus was sharp in the air and I had again that familiar sense of having left the bright coast and entered a darker country. The black outline of the Waianae Range seemed obscurely oppressive. A foursome on the post golf course seemed to have been playing since 1940, and to be doomed to continue. A soldier in fatigues appeared to be trimming a bougainvillea hedge, swinging at it with a scythe, but his movements were hypnotically slowed, and the scythe never quite touched the hedge. Around the tropical frame bungalows where the families of Schofield officers have always lived there was an occasional tricycle but no child, no wife, no sign of life but one: a Yorkshire terrier yapping on the lawn of a colonel's bungalow. As it happens I have spent time around Army posts in the role of an officer's child, have even played with lap dogs on the lawns of colonels' quarters, but I saw this Yorkshire with Prewitt's eyes, and I hated it.

I had driven out to Schofield in other seasons, but this trip was different. I was making this trip for the same reason I had walked the Oxford graveyard, a courtesy call on the owner. This trip I made appointments, spoke to people, asked questions and wrote down answers, had lunch with my hosts at the Aloha Lightning NCO Club and was shown the regimental trophies and studied the portraits of commanding officers in every corridor I walked down. Unlike the golden children in the Honolulu bookstores these men I met at Schofield, these men in green fatigues, all knew exactly who James Jones was and what he had written and even where he had slept and eaten and probably gotten drunk during the three years he spent at Schofield. They recalled the incidents and locations of *From Here to Eternity* in minute detail. They anticipated those places that I would of course want to see: D Quad, the old stockade, the stone quarry, Kolekole Pass. Some weeks before, there had been at the post theater a special screening of the movie *From Here to Eternity,* an event arranged by the Friends of the Tropic Lightning Historical Society, and everyone to whom I spoke at Schofield had turned out for this screening. Many of these men were careful to qualify their obvious attachment to James Jones's view of their life by pointing out that the Army had changed. Others did not mention the change. One, a young man who had re-upped once and now wanted out, mentioned that it had not changed at all. We were standing on the lawn in D Quad, Jones's quad, Robert E. Lee Prewitt's quad, and I was watching the idle movement around the square, a couple of soldiers dropping a basketball through a hoop, another cleaning an M-16, a desultory argument at the Dutch door of the supply room—when he volunteered a certain inchoate dissatisfaction with his six years in the 25th Division. "I read this book *From Here to Eternity,*" he said, "and they still got the same little games around here."

I suppose everything had changed and nothing had. A mess hall was now called a "dining facility," but they still served chipped beef on toast and they still called it "S.O.S." A stockade was now called a "confinement facility," and the confinement facility for all military installations on Oahu was now at Pearl Harbor, but the old stockade at Schofield was now the headquarters for the military police, and during the time I was there the M.P.s brought in a handcuffed soldier, bare to the waist and shoeless. Investigators in aloha shirts chatted in the exercise yard. Office supplies were stored in some of the "close confinement" cells, but there were still the plain wooden bunks, "plate beds,"

beds for those occasions, it was explained to me by a major who had once been in charge of the Schofield stockade, "when a guy is completely berserk and starts ripping up his mattress." On the wall there were still the diagrams detailing the order in which belongings were to be arranged: WHITE TOWEL, SOAP WITH DISH, DEODORANT, TOOTHPASTE, TOOTHBRUSH, COMB, SHAVING CREAM, RAZOR.

In many ways I found it difficult to leave Schofield that day. I had fallen into the narcoleptic movements of the Army day. I had picked up the liquid speech patterns of the Army voice. I took a copy of the *Tropic Lightning News* back into Honolulu with me, and read it that night in my hotel room. During the month of May the Schofield military police had reported 32 arrests for driving under the influence of alcohol, 115 arrests for possession of marijuana, and the theft of a number of items, including one Sansui amplifier, one Sansui pre-amp and tuner, one Kenwood receiver and turntable, two Bose speakers and the tachometer from a 1969 Ford Mustang. One private, two spec fours and one sergeant were asked in the "Troop Talk" column to name their ideal, or favorite, post. One chose Fort Hood. Another chose Fort Sam Houston. None chose Schofield Barracks. In the letters column one correspondent advised a WAC who had objected to the shows at the NCO Club to stay home ("We once had it set up where you girls didn't have to see the entertainment, but the loverly libbers put an end to that"), and another advised "barracks rats" to stop limiting their lives to "erasing Army hatred by indulging in smoke or drink or listening to Peter Frampton at eighty decibels." I thought about barracks rats and I thought about Prewitt and Maggio and I thought about Army hatred and it seemed to me that night in Honolulu that only the details had changed, that James Jones had known a great simple truth: the Army was nothing more or less than life itself. I wish I could tell you that on the day in May when James Jones died someone had played a taps for him at Schofield Barracks, but I think this is not the way life goes.

1969–1977

In Hollywood

"You can take Hollywood for granted like I did," Cecilia Brady tells the reader in *The Last Tycoon*, "or you can dismiss it with the contempt we reserve for what we don't understand. It can be understood, too, but only dimly and in flashes. Not half a dozen men have ever been able to keep the whole equation of pictures in their heads." To the extent that *The Last Tycoon* is "about" Hollywood it is about not Monroe Stahr but Cecilia Brady, as anyone who understands the equation of pictures even dimly or in flashes would apprehend immediately: the Monroe Stahrs come and go, but the Cecilia Bradys are the second generation, the survivors, the inheritors of a community as intricate, rigid, and deceptive in its mores as any devised on this continent. At midwinter in the survivors' big houses off Benedict Canyon the fireplaces blaze all day with scrub oak and eucalyptus, the French windows are opened wide to the subtropical sun, the rooms filled with white phalaenopsis and cymbidium orchids and needlepoint rugs and the requisite scent of Rigaud candles. Dinner guests pick with vermeil forks at broiled fish and limestone lettuce *vinaigrette*, decline dessert, adjourn to the screening room, and settle down to *The Heartbreak Kid* with a little seltzer in a Baccarat glass.

After the picture the women, a significant number of whom seem to have ascended through chronic shock into an elusive dottiness, discuss for a ritual half-hour the transpolar movements of acquaintances and the peace of spirit to be derived from exercise class, ballet class, the use of paper napkins at the beach. Quentin Bell's *Virginia Woolf* was an approved event this winter, as were the Chinese acrobats, the recent visits to Los Angeles of Bianca Jagger, and the opening in Beverly Hills of a branch Bonwit Teller. The men talk pictures, grosses, the deal, the morning line on the talent. "Face it," I heard someone say the other night of a director whose current picture had opened a few days before to tepid business. "Last week he was bankable."

Such evenings end before midnight. Such couples leave together. Should there be marital unhappiness it will go unmentioned until one of the principals is seen lunching with a lawyer. Should there be illness it will go unadmitted until the onset of the terminal coma. Discretion is "good taste," and discretion is also good business, since there are enough imponderables in the business of Hollywood without handing the dice to players too distracted to concentrate on the action. This is a community whose notable excesses include virtually none of the flesh or spirit: heterosexual adultery is less easily tolerated than respectably settled homosexual marriages or well-managed liaisons between middle-aged women. "A nice lesbian relationship, the most common thing in the world," I recall Otto Preminger insisting when my husband and I expressed doubt that the heroine of the Preminger picture we were writing should have one. "Very easy to arrange, does not threaten the marriage."

Flirtations between men and women, like drinks after dinner, remain largely the luxury of character actors out from New York, one-shot writers, reviewers being courted by Industry people, and others who do not understand the *mise* of the local *scène*. In the houses of the inheritors the preservation of the community is paramount, and it is also Universal, Columbia, Fox, Metro, and Warner's. It is in this tropism toward survival that Hollywood sometimes presents the appearance of the last extant stable society.

One afternoon not long ago, at a studio where my husband was doing some work, the director of a picture in production collapsed of cardiac arrest. At six o'clock the director's condition was under discussion in the executives' steam room.

"I called the hospital," the head of production for the studio said. "I talked to his wife."

"Hear what Dick did," one of the other men in the steam room commanded. "Wasn't that a nice thing for Dick to do."

This story illustrates many elements of social reality in Hollywood, but few of the several non-Industry people to whom I have told it have understood it. For one thing it involves a "studio," and many people outside the Industry are gripped by the delusion that "studios" have nothing to do with the making of motion pictures in modern times. They have heard the phrase "independent production," and have fancied that the phrase means what the words mean. They have been told about "runaways," about "empty sound stages," about "death knell" after "death knell" sounding for the Industry.

In fact the byzantine but very efficient economics of the business render such rhetoric even more meaningless than it sounds: the studios still put up almost all the money. The studios still control all effective distribution. In return for financing and distributing the average "independent" picture, the studio gets not only the largest share (at least half) of any profit made by the picture, but, more significantly, 100 per cent of what the picture brings in up to a point called the "break," or break-even, an arbitrary figure usually set at 2.7 or 2.8 times the actual, or "negative," cost of the picture.

Most significant of all, the "break-even" never represents the point at which the studio actually breaks even on any given production: that point occurs, except on paper, long before, since the studio has already received 10 to 25 per cent of the picture's budget as an "overhead" charge, has received additional rental and other fees for any services actually rendered the production company, and continues to receive, throughout the picture's release, a fee amounting to about a third of the picture's income as a "distribution" charge. In other words there is considerable income hidden in the risk itself, and the ideal picture from the studio's point of view is often said to be the picture that makes one dollar less than break-even. More perfect survival bookkeeping has been devised, but mainly in Chicago and Las Vegas.

Still, it is standard for anyone writing about Hollywood to slip out of the economic reality and into a catchier metaphor, usually paleontological, *vide* John Simon: "I shall not rehearse here the well-known facts of how the industry started dying from being too bulky, toothless, and dated—just like all those other saurians of a few aeons ago. . . ." So pervasive is this vocabulary of extinction (Simon forgot the mandatory illusion to the La Brea Tar Pits) that I am frequently assured by visitors that the studios are "morgues," that they are "shuttered up," that in "the new Hollywood" the "studio has no power." The studio has.

January in the last extant stable society. I know that it is January for an empirical fact only because wild mustard glazes the hills an acid yellow, and because there are poinsettias in front of all the bungalows down around Goldwyn and Technicolor, and because many people from Beverly Hills are at La Costa and Palm Springs and many people from New York are at the Beverly Hills Hotel.

"This whole town's dead," one such New York visitor tells me. "I dropped into the Polo Lounge last night, the place was a wasteland." He tells me this every January, and every January I tell him that people who live and work here do not frequent hotel bars either before or after dinner, but he seems to prefer his version. On reflection I can think of only three non-Industry people in New York whose version of Hollywood corresponds at any point with the reality of the place, and they are Johanna Mankiewicz Davis, Jill Schary Robinson and Jean Stein vanden Heuvel, the daughters respectively of the late screenwriter Herman Mankiewicz; the producer and former production chief at Metro, Dore Schary; and the founder of the Music Corporation of America and Universal Pictures, Jules Stein. "We don't go for strangers in Hollywood," Cecilia Brady said.

Days pass. Visitors arrive, scout the Polo Lounge, and leave, confirmed in their conviction that they have penetrated an artfully camouflaged disaster area. The morning mail contains a statement from 20th Century-Fox on a picture in which my husband and I are supposed to have "points," or a percentage. The picture cost $1,367,224.57. It has so far grossed $947,494.86. The statement might suggest to the casual subtracter that the picture is about $400,000 short of breaking even, but this is not the case: the statement reports that the picture is $1,389,112.72 short of breaking even. "$1,389,112.72 unrecovered" is, literally, the bottom line.

In lieu of contemplating why a venture that cost a million-three and has recovered almost a million remains a million-three in the red, I decide to get my hair cut, pick up the trades, learn that *The Poseidon Adventure* is grossing four million dollars a week, that Adolph "Papa" Zukor will celebrate his 100th birthday at a dinner sponsored by Paramount, and that James Aubrey, Ted Ashley and Freddie Fields rented a house together in Acapulco over Christmas. At this moment in the action, James Aubrey is Metro-Goldwyn-Mayer. Ted Ashley is Warner Brothers. Freddie Fields is Creative Management Associates, First Artists and the Directors Company. The players will change but the game will stay the same. The bottom line seems clear on the survival of Adolph "Papa" Zukor, but not yet on that of James Aubrey, Ted Ashley and Freddie Fields.

"Listen, I got this truly beautiful story," the man who cuts my hair says to me. "Think about some new Dominique-Sanda-type unknown. *Comprenez* so far?"

So far *comprends*. The man who cuts my hair, like everyone else in the community, is looking for the action, the game, a few chips to lay down. Here in the grand casino no one needs capital. One needs only this truly beautiful story. Or maybe if no truly beautiful story comes to mind one needs $500 to go halves on a

$1,000 option payment for someone else's truly beautiful but (face it) three-year-old property. (A book or a story is a "property" only until the deal; after that it is "the basic material," as in "I haven't read the basic material on *Gatsby*.") True, the casino is not now so wide open as it was in '69, summer and fall of '69 when every studio in town was narcotized by *Easy Rider*'s grosses and all that was needed to get a picture off the ground was the suggestion of a $750,000 budget, a low-cost NABET or even a nonunion crew, and this terrific 22-year-old kid director. As it turned out most of these pictures were shot as usual by IATSE rather than NABET crews and they cost as usual not seven-fifty but a million-two and many of them ended up unreleased, shelved. And so there was one very bad summer there, the hangover summer of 1970, when nobody could get past the gate without a commitment from Barbra Streisand.

That was the summer when all the terrific 22-year-old directors went back to shooting television commercials and all the creative 24-year-old producers used up the leases on their office space at Warner Brothers by sitting out there in the dull Burbank sunlight smoking dope before lunch and running one another's unreleased pictures after lunch. But that period is over and the game is back on, development money available, the deal dependent only upon the truly beautiful story and the right elements. The elements matter. "We like the *elements*," they say at studios when they are maybe going to make the deal. That is why the man who cuts my hair is telling me his story. A writer might be an element. I listen because in certain ways I am a captive but willing audience, not only to the hairdresser but at the grand casino.

The place makes everyone a gambler. Its spirit is

speedy, obsessive, immaterial. The action itself is the art form, and is described in aesthetic terms: "A very imaginative deal," they say, or, "He writes the most creative deals in the business." There is in Hollywood, as in all cultures in which gambling is the central activity, a lowered sexual energy, an inability to devote more than token attention to the preoccupations of the society outside. The action is everything, more consuming than sex, more immediate than politics; more important always than the acquisition of money, which is never, for the gambler, the true point of the exercise.

I talk on the telephone to an agent, who tells me that he has on his desk a check made out to a client for $1,275,000, the client's share of first profits on a picture now in release. Last week, in someone's office, I was shown another such check, this one made out for $4,850,000. Every year there are a few such checks around town. An agent will speak of such a check as being "on my desk," or "on Guy McElwaine's desk," as if the exact physical location lent the piece of paper its credibility. One year they might be the *Midnight Cowboy* and *Butch Cassidy* checks, another year the *Love Story* and *Godfather* checks.

In a curious way these checks are not "real," not real money in the sense that a check for a thousand dollars can be real money; no one "needs" $4,850,000, nor is it really disposable income. It is instead the unexpected payoff on dice rolled a year or two before, and its reality is altered not only by the time lapse but by the fact that no one ever counted on the payoff. A four-million-dollar windfall has the aspect only of Monopoly money, but the actual pieces of paper which bear such figures have, in the community, a totemic significance. They are totems of the action. When I hear of these totems I think reflexively of Sergius O'Shaugnessy, who sometimes believed what he said and tried to take the cure in the very real sun of Desert D'Or with its cactus, its mountain, and the bright green foliage of its love and its money.

Since any survivor is believed capable in the community of conferring on others a ritual and lucky kinship, the birthday dinner for Adolph "Papa" Zukor turns out also to have a totemic significance. It is described by Robert Evans, head of production at Paramount, as "one of the memorable evenings in our Industry. . . . There's never been anyone who's reached one hundred before." Hit songs from old Paramount pictures are played throughout dinner. Jack Valenti speaks of the guest of honor as "the motion picture world's living proof that there is a connection between us and our past."

Zukor himself, who is described in *Who's Who* as a "motion picture mfr." and in *Daily Variety* as a "firm believer in the philosophy that today is the first day of the rest of your life," appears after dinner to express his belief in the future of motion pictures and his pleasure at Paramount's recent grosses. Many of those present have had occasion over the years to regard Adolph "Papa" Zukor with some rancor, but on this night there is among them a resigned warmth, a recognition that they will attend one another's funerals. This ceremonial healing of old and recent scars is a way of life among the survivors, as is the scarring itself. "Having some fun" is what the scarring is called. "Let's go see Nick, I think we'll have some fun," David O. Selznick remembered his father saying to him when the elder Selznick was on his way to tell Nick Schenk that he was going to take 50 per cent of the gross of *Ben-Hur* away from him.

The winter progresses. My husband and I fly to Tucson with our daughter for a few days of meetings on a script with a producer on location. We go out to dinner in Tucson: the sitter tells me that she has obtained, for her crippled son, an autographed picture of Paul Newman. I ask how old her son is. "Thirty-four," she says.

We came for two days, we stay for four. We rarely leave the Hilton Inn. For everyone on the picture this life on location will continue for twelve weeks. The producer and the director collect Navajo belts and speak every day to Los Angeles, New York, London. They are setting up other deals, other action. By the time this picture is released and reviewed they will be on location in other cities. A picture in release is gone. A picture in release tends to fade from the minds of the people who made it. As the four-million-dollar check is only the totem of the action, the picture itself is in many ways only the action's by-product. "We can have some fun with this one," the producer says as we leave Tucson. "Having some fun" is also what the action itself is called.

I pass along these notes by way of suggesting that much of what is written about pictures and about picture people approaches reality only occasionally and accidentally. At one time the assurance with which many writers about film palmed off their misconceptions puzzled me a good deal. I used to wonder how

Pauline Kael, say, could slip in and out of such airy subordinate clauses as "now that the studios are collapsing," or how she could so misread the labyrinthine propriety of Industry evenings as to characterize "Hollywood wives" as women "whose jaws get a hard set from the nights when they sit soberly at parties waiting to take their sloshed geniuses home." (This fancy, oddly enough, cropped up in a review of *Alex in Wonderland,* a Paul Mazursky picture which, whatever its faults, portrayed with meticulous accuracy that level of "young" Hollywood on which the average daily narcotic intake is one glass of a three-dollar Mondavi white and two marijuana cigarettes shared by six people.) These "sloshed" husbands and "collapsing" studios derive less from Hollywood life than from some weird West Side *Playhouse 90* about Hollywood life, presumably the same one Stanley Kauffmann runs on his mind's screen when he speaks of a director like John Huston as "corrupted by success."

What is there to be said about this particular cast of mind? Some people who write about film seem so temperamentally at odds with what both Fellini and Truffaut have called the "circus" aspect of making film that there is flatly no question of their ever apprehending the social or emotional reality of the process. In this connection I think particularly of Kauffmann, whose idea of a nasty disclosure about the circus is to reveal that the aerialist is up there to get our attention. I recall him advising his readers that Otto Preminger (the same Otto Preminger who cast Joseph Welch in *Anatomy of a Murder* and engaged Louis Nizer to write a script about the Rosenbergs) was a "commercial showman," and also letting them know that he was wise to the "phoniness" in the chase sequence in *Bullitt:* "Such a chase through the normal streets of San Francisco would have ended in deaths much sooner than it does."

A curious thing about Kauffmann is that in both his dogged rightmindedness and his flatulent diction he is indistinguishable from many members of the Industry itself. He is a man who finds R. D. Laing "blazingly humane." Lewis Mumford is "civilized and civilizing" and someone to whom we owe a "long debt," Arthur Miller a "tragic agonist" hampered in his artistry only by "the shackles of our time." It is the vocabulary of the Jean Hersholt Humanitarian Award. Kauffmann divined in *Bullitt* not only its "phoniness" but a "possible propagandistic motive": "to show (particularly to the young) that law and order are not necessarily Dullsville." The "motive" in *Bullitt* was to show that several million people would pay three dollars apiece to watch Steve McQueen drive fast, but Kauffmann, like my acquaintance who reports from the Polo Lounge, seems to prefer his version. "People in the East pretend to be interested in how pictures are made," Scott Fitzgerald observed in his notes on Hollywood. "But if you actually tell them anything, you find . . . they never see the ventriloquist for the doll. Even the intellectuals, who ought to know better, like to hear about the pretensions, extravagances and vulgarities—tell them pictures have a private grammar, like politics or automobile production or society, and watch the blank look come into their faces."

Of course there is good reason for this blank look, for this almost queasy uneasiness with pictures. To recognize that the picture is but the by-product of the action is to make rather more arduous the task of maintaining one's self-image as (Kauffmann's own job definition) "a critic of new works." Making judgments on films is in many ways so peculiarly vaporous an occupation that the only question is why, beyond the obvious opportunities for a few lecture fees and a little careerism at a dispiritingly self-limiting level, anyone does it in the first place. A finished picture defies all attempts to analyze what makes it work or not work: the responsibility for its every frame is clouded not only in the accidents and compromises of production but in the clauses of its financing. *The Getaway* was Sam Peckinpah's picture, but Steve McQueen had the "cut," or final right to edit. *Up the Sandbox* was Irvin Kershner's picture, but Barbra Streisand had the cut. In a series of interviews with directors, Charles Thomas Samuels asked Carol Reed why he had used the same cutter on so many pictures. "I had no control," Reed said. Samuels asked Vittorio De Sica if he did not find a certain effect in one of his Sophia Loren films a bit artificial. "It was shot by the second unit," De Sica said. "I didn't direct it." In other words, Carlo Ponti wanted it.

Nor does calling film a "collaborative medium" exactly describe the situation. To read David O. Selznick's instructions to his directors, writers, actors and department heads in *Memo from David O. Selznick* is to come very close to the spirit of actually making a picture, a spirit not of collaboration but of armed conflict in which one antagonist has a contract assuring him nuclear capability. Some reviewers make a point of trying to understand whose picture it is by "looking at the script": to understand whose picture it is one needs to look not particularly at the script but at the deal memo.

About the best a writer on film can hope to do, then, is to bring an engaging or interesting intelligence to bear upon the subject, a kind of *petit-point*-on-Kleenex effect which rarely stands much scrutiny. "Motives" are inferred where none existed; allegations spun out of thin speculation. Perhaps the difficulty of knowing who made which choices in a picture makes this airiness so expedient that it eventually infects any writer who makes a career of reviewing; perhaps the initial error is in making a career of it. Reviewing motion pictures, like reviewing new cars, may or may not be a useful consumer service (since people respond to a lighted screen in a dark room in the same secret and powerfully irrational way they respond to most sensory stimuli, I tend to think much of it beside the point, but never mind that); the review of pictures has been, as well, a traditional diversion for writers whose actual work is somewhere else. Some 400 mornings spent at press screenings in the late Thirties were, for Graham Greene, an "escape," a way of life "adopted quite voluntarily from a sense of fun." Perhaps it is only when one inflates this sense of fun into (Kauffmann again) "a continuing relation with an art" that one passes so headily beyond the reality principle.

February in the last extant stable society. A few days ago I went to lunch in Beverly Hills. At the next table were an agent and a director who should have been, at that moment, on his way to a location to begin a new picture. I knew what he was supposed to be doing because this picture had been talked about around town: six million dollars above the line. There was two million for one actor. There was a million and a quarter for another actor. The director was in for $800,000. The property had cost more than half a million; the first-draft screenplay $200,000, the second draft a little less. A third writer had been brought in, at $6,000 a week. Among the three writers were two Academy Awards and one New York Film Critics Award. The director had an Academy Award for his last picture but one.

And now the director was sitting at lunch in Beverly Hills and he wanted out. The script was not right. Only 38 pages worked, the director said. The financing was shaky. "They're in breach, we all recognize your right to pull out," the agent said carefully. The agent represented many of the principals, and did not want the director to pull out. On the other hand he also represented the director, and the director seemed unhappy. It was difficult to ascertain what anyone involved did want, except for the action to continue. "You pull out," the agent said, "it dies right here, not that I want to influence your decision." The director picked up the bottle of Margaux they were drinking and examined the label.

"Nice little red," the agent said.

"Very nice."

I left as the Sanka was being served. No decision had been reached. Many people have been talking these past few days about this aborted picture, always with a note of regret. It had been a very creative deal and they had run with it as far as they could run and they had had some fun and now the fun was over, as it also would have been had they made the picture.

1973

In Bed

THREE, FOUR, sometimes five times a month, I spend the day in bed with a migraine headache, insensible to the world around me. Almost every day of every month, between these attacks, I feel the sudden irrational irritation and the flush of blood into the cerebral arteries which tell me that migraine is on its way, and I take certain drugs to avert its arrival. If I did not take the drugs, I would be able to function perhaps one day in four. The physiological error called migraine is, in brief, central to the given of my life. When I was 15, 16, even 25, I used to think that I could rid myself of this error by simply denying it, character over chemistry. "Do you have headaches *sometimes? frequently? never?*" the application forms would demand. "Check one." Wary of the trap, wanting whatever it was that the successful circumnavigation of that particular form could bring (a job, a scholarship, the respect of mankind and the grace of God), I would check one. "*Sometimes,*" I would lie. That in fact I spent one or two days a week almost unconscious with pain seemed a shameful secret, evidence not merely of some chemical inferiority but of all my bad attitudes, unpleasant tempers, wrongthink.

For I had no brain tumor, no eyestrain, no high blood pressure, nothing wrong with me at all: I simply had migraine headaches, and migraine headaches were, as everyone who did not have them knew, imaginary. I fought migraine then, ignored the warnings it sent, went to school and later to work in spite of it, sat through lectures in Middle English and presentations to advertisers with involuntary tears running down the right side of my face, threw up in washrooms, stumbled home by instinct, emptied ice trays onto my bed and tried to freeze the pain in my right temple, wished only for a neurosurgeon who would do a lobotomy on house call, and cursed my imagination.

It was a long time before I began thinking mechanistically enough to accept migraine for what it was: something with which I would be living, the way some people live with diabetes. Migraine is something more than the fancy of a neurotic imagination. It is an essentially hereditary complex of symptoms, the most frequently noted but by no means the most unpleasant of which is a vascular headache of blinding severity, suffered by a surprising number of women, a fair number of men (Thomas Jefferson had migraine, and so did Ulysses S. Grant, the day he accepted Lee's surrender), and by some unfortunate children as young as two years old. (I had my first when I was eight. It came on during a fire drill at the Columbia School in Colorado Springs, Colorado. I was taken first home and then to the infirmary at Peterson Field, where my father was stationed. The Air Corps doctor prescribed an enema.) Almost anything can trigger a specific attack of migraine: stress, allergy, fatigue, an abrupt change in barometric pressure, a contretemps over a parking ticket. A flashing light. A fire drill. One inherits, of course, only the predisposition. In other words I spent yesterday in bed with a headache not merely because of my bad attitudes, unpleasant tempers and wrongthink, but because both my grandmothers had migraine, my father has migraine and my mother has migraine.

No one knows precisely what it is that is inherited. The chemistry of migraine, however, seems to have some connection with the nerve hormone named serotonin, which is naturally present in the brain. The amount of serotonin in the blood falls sharply at the onset of migraine, and one migraine drug, methysergide, or Sansert, seems to have some effect on serotonin. Methysergide is a derivative of lysergic acid (in fact Sandoz Pharmaceuticals first synthesized LSD-25 while looking for a migraine cure), and its use is hemmed about with so many contraindications and side effects that most doctors prescribe it only in the most incapacitating cases. Methysergide, when it is prescribed, is taken daily, as a preventive; another preventive which works for some people is old-fashioned ergotamine tartrate, which helps to constrict the swelling blood vessels during the "aura," the period which in most cases precedes the actual headache.

Once an attack is under way, however, no drug touches it. Migraine gives some people mild hallucinations, temporarily blinds others, shows up not only as a headache but as a gastrointestinal disturbance, a painful sensitivity to all sensory stimuli, an abrupt overpowering fatigue, a strokelike aphasia, and a crippling inability to make even the most routine connections. When I am in a migraine aura (for some people the aura lasts fifteen minutes, for others several hours), I will drive through red lights, lose the house keys, spill whatever I am holding, lose the ability to focus my eyes or frame coherent sentences, and generally give the appearance of being on drugs, or drunk. The actual headache, when it comes, brings with it chills, sweating, nausea, a debility that seems to stretch the very limits of endurance. That no one dies of migraine seems, to someone deep into an attack, an ambiguous blessing.

My husband also has migraine, which is unfortunate for him but fortunate for me: perhaps nothing so tends to prolong an attack as the accusing eye of someone who has never had a headache. "Why not take a couple of aspirin," the unafflicted will say from the doorway, or "I'd have a headache, too, spending a beautiful day like this inside with all the shades drawn." All of us who have migraine suffer not only from the attacks themselves but from this common conviction that we are perversely refusing to cure ourselves by taking a couple of aspirin, that we are making ourselves sick, that we "bring it on ourselves." And in the most immediate sense, the sense of why we have a headache this Tuesday and not last Thursday, of course we often do. There certainly is what doctors call a "migraine personality," and that personality tends to be ambitious, inward, intolerant of error, rather rigidly organized, perfectionist. "You don't look like a migraine personality," a doctor once said to me. "Your hair's messy. But I suppose you're a compulsive housekeeper." Actually my house is kept even more negligently than my hair, but the doctor was right nonetheless: perfectionism can also take the form of spending most of a week writing and rewriting and not writing a single paragraph.

But not all perfectionists have migraine, and not all migrainous people have migraine personalities. We do not escape heredity. I have tried in most of the available ways to escape my own migrainous heredity (at one point I learned to give myself two daily injections of histamine with a hypodermic needle, even though the needle so frightened me that I had to close my eyes when I did it), but I still have migraine. And I have learned now to live with it, learned when to expect it, how to outwit it, even how to regard it, when it does come, as more friend than lodger. We have reached a certain understanding, my migraine and I. It never comes when I am in real trouble. Tell me that my house is burned down, my husband has left me, that there is gunfighting in the streets and panic in the banks, and I will not respond by getting a headache. It comes instead when I am fighting not an open but a guerrilla war with my own life, during weeks of small household confusions, lost laundry, unhappy help, canceled appointments, on days when the telephone rings too much and I get no work done and the wind is coming up. On days like that my friend comes uninvited.

And once it comes, now that I am wise in its ways, I no longer fight it. I lie down and let it happen. At first every small apprehension is magnified, every anxiety a pounding terror. Then the pain comes, and I concentrate only on that. Right there is the usefulness of migraine, there in that imposed yoga, the concentration on the pain. For when the pain recedes, ten or twelve hours later, everything goes with it, all the hidden resentments, all the vain anxieties. The migraine has acted as a circuit breaker, and the fuses have emerged intact. There is a pleasant convalescent euphoria. I open the windows and feel the air, eat gratefully, sleep well. I notice the particular nature of a flower in a glass on the stair landing. I count my blessings.

1968

On the Road

Where are we heading, they asked in all the television and radio studios. They asked it in New York and Los Angeles and they asked it in Boston and Washington and they asked it in Dallas and Houston and Chicago and San Francisco. Sometimes they made eye contact as they asked it. Sometimes they closed their eyes as they asked it. Quite often they wondered not just where we were heading but where we were heading "as Americans," or "as concerned Americans," or "as American women," or, on one occasion, "as the American guy and the American woman." I never learned the answer, nor did the answer matter, for one of the eerie and liberating aspects of broadcast discourse is that nothing one says will alter in the slightest either the form or the length of the conversation. Our voices in the studios were those of manic actors assigned to do three-minute, four-minute, seven-minute improvs. Our faces on the monitors were those of concerned Americans. On my way to one of those studios in Boston I had seen the magnolias bursting white down Marlborough Street. On my way to another in Dallas I had watched the highway lights blazing and dimming pink against the big dawn sky. Outside one studio in Houston the afternoon heat was sinking into the deep primeval green of the place and outside the next, that night in Chicago, snow fell and glittered in the lights along the lake. Outside all these studios America lay in all its exhilaratingly volatile weather and eccentricity and specificity, but inside the studios we shed the specific and rocketed on to the general, for they were The Interviewers and I was The Author and the single question we seemed able to address together was *where are we heading*.

"8:30 A.M. to 9:30 A.M.: LIVE on WFSB TV/THIS MORNING.
"10 A.M. to 10:30 A.M.: LIVE on WINF AM/THE WORLD TODAY.
"10:45 A.M. to 11:45 A.M.: PRESS INTERVIEW with HARTFORD COURANT.
"12 noon to 1:30 P.M.: AUTOGRAPHING at BARNES AND NOBLE.
"2 P.M. to 2:30 P.M.: TAPE at WDRC AM/FM.
"3 P.M. to 3:30 P.M.: PRESS INTERVIEW with THE HILL INK.
"7:30 P.M. to 9 P.M.: TAPE at WHNB TV/WHAT ABOUT WOMEN."

From 12 noon to 1:30 P.M., that first day in Hartford, I talked to a man who had cut a picture of me from a magazine in 1970 and had come round to Barnes and Noble to see what I looked like in 1977. From 2 P.M. to 2:30 P.M., that first day in Hartford, I listened to the receptionists at WDRC AM/FM talk about the new records and I watched snow drop from the pine boughs in the cemetery across the street. The name of the cemetery was Mt. St. Benedict and my husband's father had been buried there. "Any Steely Dan come in?" the receptionists kept asking. From 8:30 A.M. until 9 P.M., that first day in Hartford, I neglected to mention the name of the book I was supposed to be promoting. It was my fourth book but I had never before done what is called in the trade a book tour. I was not sure what I was doing or why I was doing it. I had left California equipped with two "good" suits, a box of unanswered mail, Elizabeth Hardwick's *Seduction and Betrayal,* Edmund Wilson's *To the Finland Station,* six Judy Blume books and my eleven-year-old daughter. The Judy Blume books were along to divert my daughter. My daughter was along to divert me. Three days into the tour I sent home the box of unanswered mail to make room for a packet of Simon and Schuster press releases describing me in favorable terms. Four days into the tour I sent home *Seduction and Betrayal* and *To the Finland Station* to make room for a thousand-watt hair blower. By the time I reached Boston, ten days into the tour, I knew that I had never before heard and would possibly never again hear America singing at precisely this pitch: ethereal, speedy, an angel choir on Dexamyl.

Where were we heading. The set for this discussion was always the same: a cozy oasis of wicker and ferns in the wilderness of cables and cameras and Styrofoam coffee cups that was the actual studio. On wicker settees across the nation I expressed my conviction that we were heading "into an era" of whatever the clock seemed to demand. In green rooms across the nation I listened to other people talk about where we were heading, and also about their vocations, avocations, and secret interests. I discussed L-dopa and biorhythm with a woman whose father invented prayer breakfasts. I exchanged makeup tips with a former Mouseketeer. I stopped reading newspapers and started relying on bulletins from limo drivers, from

Mouseketeers, from the callers-in on call-in shows and from the closed-circuit screens in airports that flashed random stories off the wire ("CARTER URGES BARBITURATE BAN" is one that got my attention at La Guardia) between advertisements for *Shenandoah*. I gravitated to the random. I swung with the nonsequential.

I began to see America as my own, a child's map over which my child and I could skim and light at will. We spoke not of cities but of airports. If rain fell at Logan we could find sun at Dulles. Bags lost at O'Hare could be found at Dallas/Fort Worth. In the first-class cabins of the planes on which we traveled we were often, my child and I, the only female passengers, and I apprehended for the first time those particular illusions of mobility which power American business. Time was money. Motion was progress. Decisions were snap and the ministrations of other people were constant. Room service, for example, assumed paramount importance. We needed, my eleven-year-old and I, instant but erratically timed infusions of consommé, oatmeal, crab salad and asparagus vinaigrette. We needed Perrier water and tea to drink when we were working. We needed bourbon on the rocks and Shirley Temples to drink when we were not. A kind of irritable panic came over us when room service went off, and also when no one answered in the housekeeping department. In short we had fallen into the peculiar hormonal momentum of business travel, and I had begun to understand the habituation many men and a few women have to planes and telephones and schedules. I had begun to regard my own schedule—a sheaf of thick cream-colored pages printed with the words "SIMON & SCHUSTER/A DIVISION OF GULF & WESTERN

CORPORATION"—with a reverence approaching the mystical. We wanted 24-hour room service. We wanted direct-dial telephones. We wanted to stay on the road forever.

WE SAW AIR AS OUR ELEMENT. In Houston the air was warm and rich and suggestive of fossil fuel and we pretended we owned a house in River Oaks. In Chicago the air was brilliant and thin and we pretended we owned the 27th floor of the Ritz. In New York the air was charged and crackling and shorting out with opinions, and we pretended we had some. Everyone in New York had opinions. Opinions were demanded in return. The absence of opinion was construed as opinion. Even my daughter was developing opinions. "Had an interesting talk with Carl Bernstein," she noted in the log she had been assigned to keep for her fifth-grade teacher in Malibu, California. Many of these New York opinions seemed intended as tonic revisions, bold corrections to opinions in vogue during the previous week, but since I had just dropped from the sky it was difficult for me to distinguish those opinions which were "bold" and "revisionist" from those which were merely "weary" and "rote." At the time I left New York many people were expressing a bold belief in "joy"—joy in children, joy in wedlock, joy in the dailiness of life—but joy was trickling down fast to show-business personalities. Mike Nichols, for example, was expressing his joy in the pages of *Newsweek*, and also his weariness with "lapidary bleakness." Lapidary bleakness was definitely rote.

We were rethinking the Sixties that week, or Morris Dickstein was.

We were taking another look at the Fifties that week, or Hilton Kramer was.

I agreed passionately. I disagreed passionately. I called room service on one phone and listened attentively on the other to people who seemed convinced that the "texture" of their lives had been agreeably or adversely affected by conversion to the politics of joy, by regression to lapidary bleakness, by the Sixties, by the Fifties, by the recent change in administrations and by the sale of *The Thorn Birds* to paper for one-million-nine.

I lost track of information.

I was blitzed by opinion.

I began to see opinions arcing in the air, intersecting flight patterns. The Eastern shuttle was cleared for landing and so was lapidary bleakness. John Leonard and joy were on converging vectors. I began to see the country itself as a projection on air, a kind of hologram, an invisible grid of image and opinion and electronic impulse. There were opinions in the air and there were planes in the air and there were even people in the air: one afternoon in New York my husband saw a man jump from a window and fall to the sidewalk outside the Yale Club. I mentioned this to a *Daily News* photographer who was taking my picture. "You have to catch a jumper in the act to make the paper," he advised me. He had caught two in the act but only the first had made the paper. The second was a better picture but coincided with the crash of a DC-10 at Orly. "They're all over town," the photographer said. "Jumpers. A lot of them aren't even jumpers. They're window washers. Who fall."

What does that say about us as a nation, I was asked the next day when I mentioned the jumpers and window washers on the air. *Where are we headed.* On the 27th floor of the Ritz in Chicago my daughter and I sat frozen at the breakfast table until the window washers glided safely out of sight. At a call-in station in Los Angeles I was told by the guard that there would be a delay because they had a jumper on the line. "I say let him jump," the guard said to me. I imagined a sky dense with jumpers and fallers and DC-10s. I held my daughter's hand at takeoff and landing and watched for antennae on the drive into town. The big antennae with the pulsing red lights had been for a month our landmarks. The big antennae with the pulsing red lights had in fact been for a month our destinations. "Out I-10 to the antenna" was the kind of direction we had come to understand, for we were on the road, on the grid, on the air and also in it. *Where were we heading.* I don't know where you're heading, I said in the studio attached to the last of these antennae, my eyes fixed on still another of the neon FLEETWOOD MAC signs that flickered that spring in radio stations from coast to coast, but I'm heading home.

1977

On the Mall

THEY FLOAT on the landscape like pyramids to the boom years, all those Plazas and Malls and Esplanades. All those Squares and Fairs. All those Towns and Dales, all those Villages, all those Forests and Parks and Lands. Stonestown. Hillsdale. Valley Fair, Mayfair, Northgate, Southgate, Eastgate, Westgate. Gulfgate. They are toy garden cities in which no one lives but everyone consumes, profound equalizers, the perfect fusion of the profit motive and the egalitarian ideal, and to hear their names is to recall words and phrases no longer quite current. Baby Boom. Consumer Explosion. Leisure Revolution. Do-It-Yourself Revolution. Backyard Revolution. Suburbia. "The Shopping Center," the Urban Land Institute could pronounce in 1957, "is today's extraordinary retail business evolvement. . . . The automobile accounts for suburbia, and suburbia accounts for the shopping center."

It was a peculiar and visionary time, those years after World War II to which all the Malls and Towns and Dales stand as climate-controlled monuments. Even the word "automobile," as in "the automobile accounts for suburbia and suburbia accounts for the shopping center," no longer carries the particular freight it once did: as a child in the late Forties in California I recall reading and believing that the "freedom of movement" afforded by the automobile was "America's fifth freedom." The trend was up. The solution was in sight. The frontier had been reinvented, and its shape was the subdivision, that new free land on which all settlers could recast their lives *tabula rasa*. For one perishable moment there the American idea seemed about to achieve itself, via F.H.A. housing and the acquisition of major appliances, and a certain enigmatic glamour attached to the architects of this newfound land. They made something of nothing. They gambled and sometimes lost. They staked the past to seize the future. I have difficulty now imagining a childhood in which a man named Jere Strizek, the developer of Town and Country Village outside Sacramento (143,000 square feet gross floor area, 68 stores, 1000 parking spaces, the Urban Land Institute's "prototype for centers using heavy timber and tile construction for informality"), could materialize as a role model, but I had such a childhood, just after World War II, in Sacramento. I never met or even saw Jere Strizek, but at the age of 12 I imagined him a kind of frontiersman, a romantic and revolutionary spirit, and in the indigenous grain he was.

I suppose James B. Douglas and David D. Bohannon were too.

I first heard of James B. Douglas and David D. Bohannon not when I was 12 but a dozen years later, when I was living in New York, working for *Vogue*, and taking, by correspondence, a University of California Extension course in shopping-center theory. This did not seem to me eccentric at the time. I remember sitting on the cool floor in Irving Penn's studio and reading, in *The Community Builders Handbook*, advice from James B.

Douglas on shopping-center financing. I recall staying late in my pale-blue office on the twentieth floor of the Graybar Building to memorize David D. Bohannon's parking ratios. My "real" life was to sit in this office and describe life as it was lived in Djakarta and Caneel Bay and in the great châteaux of the Loire Valley, but my dream life was to put together a Class-A regional shopping center with three full-line department stores as major tenants.

That I was perhaps the only person I knew in New York, let alone on the Condé Nast floors of the Graybar Building, to have memorized the distinctions among "A," "B," and "C" shopping centers did not occur to me (the defining distinction, as long as I have your attention, is that an "A," or "regional," center has as its major tenant a full-line department store which carries major appliances; a "B," or "community," center has as its major tenant a junior department store which does not carry major appliances; and a "C," or "neighborhood," center has as its major tenant only a supermarket): my interest in shopping centers was in no way casual. I did want to build them. I wanted to build them because I had fallen into the habit of writing fiction, and I had it in my head that a couple of good centers might support this habit less taxingly than a pale-blue office at *Vogue*. I had even devised an original scheme by which I planned to gain enough capital and credibility to enter the shopping-center game: I would lease warehouses in, say, Queens, and offer Manhattan delicatessens the opportunity to sell competitively by buying cooperatively, from my trucks. I see a few wrinkles in this scheme now (the words "concrete overcoat" come to mind), but I did not then. In fact I planned to run it out of the pale-blue office.

James B. Douglas and David D. Bohannon. In 1950 James B. Douglas had opened Northgate, in Seattle, the first regional center to combine a pedestrian mall with an underground truck tunnel. In 1954 David D. Bohannon had opened Hillsdale, a forty-acre regional center on the peninsula south of San Francisco. That is the only solid bio I have on James B. Douglas and David D. Bohannon to this day, but many of their opinions are engraved on my memory. David D. Bohannon believed in preserving the integrity of the shopping center by not cutting up the site with any dedicated roads. David D. Bohannon believed that architectural setbacks in a center looked "pretty on paper" but caused "customer resistance." James B. Douglas advised that a small-loan office could prosper in a center only if it was placed away from foot traffic, since people who want small loans do not want to be observed getting them. I do not now recall whether it was James B. Douglas or David D. Bohannon or someone else altogether who passed along this hint on how to paint the lines around the parking spaces (actually this is called "striping the lot," and the spaces are "stalls"): make each space a foot wider than it need be —ten feet, say, instead of nine—when the center first opens and business is slow. By this single stroke the developer achieves a couple of important objectives, the appearance of a popular center and the illusion of easy parking, and no one will really notice when business picks up and the spaces shrink.

Nor do I recall who first solved what was once a crucial center dilemma: the placement of the major tenant vis-à-vis the parking lot. The dilemma was that the major tenant—the draw, the raison d'être for the financing, the Sears, the Macy's, the May Company—

wanted its customer to walk directly from car to store. The smaller tenants, on the other hand, wanted that same customer to *pass their stores* on the way from the car to, say, Macy's. The solution to this conflict of interests was actually very simple: *two major tenants,* one at each end of a mall. This is called "anchoring the mall," and represents seminal work in shopping-center theory. One thing you will note about shopping-center theory is that you could have thought of it yourself, and a course in it will go a long way toward dispelling the notion that business proceeds from mysteries too recondite for you and me.

A few aspects of shopping-center theory do in fact remain impenetrable to me. I have no idea why the Community Builders' Council ranks "Restaurant" as deserving a Number One (or "Hot Spot") location but exiles "Chinese Restaurant" to a Number Three, out there with "Power and Light Office" and "Christian Science Reading Room." Nor do I know why the Council approves of enlivening a mall with "small animals" but specifically, vehemently, and with no further explanation, excludes "monkeys." If I had a center I would have monkeys, and Chinese restaurants, and Mylar kites and bands of small girls playing tambourine.

A few years ago at a party I met a woman from Detroit who told me that the Joyce Carol Oates novel with which she identified most closely was *Wonderland.*

I asked her why.

"Because," she said, "my husband has a branch there."

I did not understand.

"In Wonderland the center," the woman said patiently. "My husband has a branch in Wonderland."

I have never visited Wonderland but imagine it to have bands of small girls playing tambourine.

A few facts about shopping centers.

The "biggest" center in the United States is generally agreed to be Woodfield, outside Chicago, a "super" regional or "leviathan" two-million-square-foot center with four major tenants.

The "first" shopping center in the United States is generally agreed to be Country Club Plaza in Kansas City, built in the twenties. There were some other early centers, notably Edward H. Bouton's 1907 Roland Park in Baltimore, Hugh Prather's 1931 Highland Park Shopping Village in Dallas, and Hugh Potter's 1937 River Oaks in Houston, but the developer of Country Club Plaza, the late J. C. Nichols, is referred to with ritual frequency in the literature of shopping centers, usually as "pioneering J. C. Nichols," "trailblazing J. C. Nichols," or "J. C. Nichols, father of the center as we know it."

Those are some facts I know about shopping centers because I still want to be Jere Strizek or James B. Douglas or David D. Bohannon. Here are some facts I know about shopping centers because I never will be Jere Strizek or James B. Douglas or David D. Bohannon: a good center in which to spend the day if you wake feeling low in Honolulu, Hawaii, is Ala Moana, major tenants Liberty House and Sears. A good center in which to spend the day if you wake feeling low in Oxnard, California, is The Esplanade, major tenants the

May Company and Sears. A good center in which to spend the day if you wake feeling low in Biloxi, Mississippi, is Edgewater Plaza, major tenant Godchaux's. Ala Moana in Honolulu is larger than The Esplanade in Oxnard, and The Esplanade in Oxnard is larger than Edgewater Plaza in Biloxi. Ala Moana has carp pools. The Esplanade and Edgewater Plaza do not.

These marginal distinctions to one side, Ala Moana, The Esplanade, and Edgewater Plaza are the same place, which is precisely their role not only as equalizers but in the sedation of anxiety. In each of them one moves for a while in an aqueous suspension not only of light but of judgment, not only of judgment but of "personality." One meets no acquaintances at The Esplanade. One gets no telephone calls at Edgewater Plaza. "It's a hard place to run in to for a pair of stockings," a friend complained to me recently of Ala Moana, and I knew that she was not yet ready to surrender her ego to the idea of the center. The last time I went to Ala Moana it was to buy *The New York Times*. Because *The New York Times* was not in, I sat on the mall for a while and ate caramel corn. In the end I bought not *The New York Times* at all but two straw hats at Liberty House, four bottles of nail enamel at Woolworth's, and a toaster, on sale at Sears. In the literature of shopping centers these would be described as impulse purchases, but the impulse here was obscure. I do not wear hats, nor do I like caramel corn. I do not use nail enamel. Yet flying back across the Pacific I regretted only the toaster.

1975

In Bogotá

On the Colombian coast it was hot, fevered, eleven degrees off the equator with evening trades that did not relieve but blew hot and dusty. The sky was white, the casino idle. I had never meant to leave the coast but after a week of it I began to think exclusively of Bogotá, floating on the Andes an hour away by air. In Bogotá it would be cool. In Bogotá one could get *The New York Times* only two days late and the *Miami Herald* only one day late and also emeralds, and bottled water. In Bogotá there would be fresh roses in the bathrooms at the Hotel Tequendama and hot water twenty-four hours a day and numbers to be dialed for chicken sandwiches from room service and Xerox *rápido* and long-distance operators who could get Los Angeles in ten minutes. In my room in Cartagena I would wake to the bleached coastal morning and find myself repeating certain words and phrases under my breath, an incantation: *Bogotá, Bacatá.* El Dorado. Emeralds. Hot water. Madeira consommé in cool dining rooms. *Santa Fé de Bogotá del Nuevo Reino de Granada de las Indias del Mar Océano.* The Avianca flight to Bogotá left Cartagena every morning at ten-forty, but such was the slowed motion of the coast that it took me another four days to get on it.

Maybe that is the one true way to see Bogotá, to have it float in the mind until the need for it is visceral, for the whole history of the place has been to seem a mirage, a delusion on the high savannah, its gold and its emeralds unattainable, inaccessible, its isolation so splendid and unthinkable that the very existence of a city astonishes. There on the very spine of the Andes gardeners espalier roses on embassy walls. Swarms of little girls in proper navy-blue school blazers line up to enter the faded tent of a tatty traveling circus: the elephant, the strong man, the tattooed man from Maracaibo. I arrived in Bogotá on a day in 1973 when the streets seemed bathed in mist and thin brilliant light and in the amplified pop voice of Nelson Ned, a Brazilian dwarf whose records played in every *disco* storefront. Outside the sixteenth-century Church of San Francisco, where the Spanish viceroys took office when the country was Nueva Granada and where Simón Bolívar assumed the presidency of the doomed republic called Gran Colombia, small children and old women hawked Cuban cigars and cartons of American cigarettes and newspapers with the headline "JACKIE Y ARI." I lit a candle for my daughter and bought a paper to read about Jackie and Ari, how the princess *de los norteamericanos* ruled the king of the Greek sea by demanding of him pink champagne every night and *medialunas* every morning, a story a child might invent. Later, in the Gold Museum of the Banco de la República, I looked at the gold the Spaniards opened the Americas to get, the vision of El Dorado which was to animate a century and is believed to have begun here, outside Bogotá, at Lake Guatavita. "Many golden offerings were cast into the lake," wrote the anthropologist Olivia Vlahos of the nights when the Chibcha Indians lit bonfires on the Andes and confirmed their rulers at Guatavita.

Many more were heaped on a raft. . . . Then into the firelight stepped the ruler-to-be, his nakedness coated with a sticky resin. Onto the resin his priests applied gold dust and more gold dust until he gleamed like a golden statue. He stepped onto the raft, which was cut loose to drift into the middle of the lake. Suddenly he dived into the black water. When he emerged, the gold was gone, washed clean from his body. And he was king.

Until the Spaniards heard the story, and came to find El Dorado for themselves. "One thing you must understand," a young Colombian said to me at dinner that night. We were at Eduardo's out in the Chico district and the piano player was playing "Love Is Blue" and we were drinking an indifferent bottle of Château Léoville-Poyferré which cost $20 American. "Spain sent all its highest aristocracy to South America." In fact I had heard variations on this hallucination before, on the coast: when Colombians spoke about the past I often had the sense of being in a place where history tended to sink, even as it happened, into the traceless solitude of autosuggestion. The princess was drinking pink champagne. High in the mountains the men were made of gold. Spain sent its highest aristocracy to South America. They were all stories a child might invent.

Many years later, as he faced the firing squad, Colonel Aureliano Buendía was to remember that distant afternoon when his father took him to discover ice.

—The opening line of *One Hundred Years of Solitude*,
by the Colombian novelist
Gabriel García Márquez.

At the big movie theaters in Bogotá in the spring of 1973 *The Professionals* was playing, and *It's a Mad Mad Mad Mad World,* two American pictures released in, respectively, 1967 and 1964. The English-language racks of paperback stands were packed with Edmund Wilson's *The Cold War and the Income Tax,* the 1964 Signet edition. This slight but definite dislocation of time fixed on the mind the awesome isolation of the place, as did dislocations of other kinds. On the fourth floor of the glossy new Bogotá Hilton one could lunch in an orchid-filled gallery that overlooked the indoor swimming pool, and also overlooked a shantytown of packing-crate and tin-can shacks where a small boy, his body hideously scarred and his face obscured by a knitted mask, played listlessly with a yo-yo. In the lobby of the Hotel Tequendama two Braniff stewardesses in turquoise-blue Pucci pantsuits flirted desultorily with a German waiting for the airport limousine; a third ignored the German and stood before a relief map on which buttons could be pressed to light up the major cities of Colombia. Santa Marta, on the coast; Barranquilla, Cartagena. Medellín, on the Central Cordillera. Cali, on the Cauca River, San Agustín on the Magdalena. Leticia, on the Amazon.

I watched her press the buttons one by one, transfixed by the vast darkness each tiny bulb illumined. The light for Bogotá blinked twice and went out. The girl in the Pucci pantsuit traced the Andes with her index finger. *Alto arrecife de la aurora humana,* the Chilean poet Pablo Neruda called the Andes. *High reef of the human dawn.* It cost the *conquistador* Gonzalo Jiménez de Quesada two years and the health of most of his men to reach Bogotá from the coast. It cost me $26.

"I knew they were your bags," the man at the airport said, producing them triumphantly from a moraine of baggage and cartons and rubble from the construction that seemed all over Bogotá a chronic condition. "They smelled American." *Parece una turista norteamericana,* I read about myself in *El Espectador* a few mornings later. She resembles an American tourist. In fact I was aware of being an American in Colombia in a way I had not been in other places. I kept running into Americans, compatriots for whom the emotional center of Bogotá was the massive concrete embassy on Carrera 10, members of a phantom colony called "the American presence" which politesse prevented them from naming out loud. Several times I met a young American who ran an "information" office, which he urged me to visit; he had extremely formal manners, appeared for the most desultory evening in black tie, and was, according to the Colombian I asked, CIA. I recall talking at a party to a USIS man who spoke in a low mellifluous voice of fevers he had known, fevers in Sierra Leone, fevers in Monrovia, fevers on the Colombian coast. Our host interrupted this litany, demanded to know why the ambassador had not come to the party. "Little situation in Cali," the USIS man said, and smiled professionally. He seemed very concerned that no breach of American manners be inferred, and so, absurdly, did I. We had nothing in common except the eagles on our passports, but those eagles made us, in some way I did not entirely understand, co-conspirators, two strangers heavy with responsibility for seeing that the eagle should not offend. We would prefer the sweet local Roman-Cola to the Coca-Cola the Colombians liked. We would think of Standard Oil as Esso Colombiano. We would not speak of fever except to one another. Later I met an American actor who had spent two weeks taking cold showers in Bogotá before he discovered that the hot and cold taps in the room assigned him were simply reversed: he had never asked, he said, because he did not want to be considered an arrogant *gringo*.

In *El Tiempo* that morning I had read that General Gustavo Rojas Pinilla, who took over Colombia in a military coup in 1953 and closed down the press before he was overthrown in 1957, was launching a new bid for power on a Peronist platform, and I had thought that perhaps people at the party would be talking about that, but they were not. Why had the American film industry not made films about the Vietnam War, was what the Colombian stringer for the Caribbean newspaper wanted to talk about. The young Colombian filmmakers looked at him incredulously. "What would be the point," one finally shrugged. "They run that war on television."

The filmmakers had lived in New York, spoke of Rip Torn, Norman Mailer, Ricky Leacock, Super 8. One had come to the party in a stovepipe preacher's hat; another in a violet macramé shawl to the knees. The girl with them, a famous beauty from the coast, wore a flamingo-pink sequinned midriff, and her pale red hair was fluffed around her head in an electric halo. She watched the *cumbia* dancers and fondled a baby ocelot and remained impassive both to the possibility of General Gustavo Rojas Pinilla's comeback and to the question of why the American film industry had not made films about the Vietnam War. Later, outside the gate, the filmmakers lit thick marijuana cigarettes in view of the uniformed *policia* and asked if I knew Paul Morrissey's and Andy Warhol's address in Rome. The girl from the coast cradled her ocelot against the wind.

Of the time I spent in Bogotá I remember mainly images, indelible but difficult to connect. I remember the walls on the second floor of the Museo Nacional, white and cool and lined with portraits of the presidents of Colombia, a great many presidents. I remember the emeralds in shop windows, lying casually in trays, all of them oddly pale at the center, somehow watered, cold at the very heart where one expects the fire. I asked the price of one: "Twenty-thousand American," the woman said. She was reading a booklet called *Horóscopo: Sagitario* and did not look up. I remember walking across Plaza Bolívar, the great square from which all Colombian power emanates, at midafternoon when men in dark European suits stood talking on the steps of the Capitol and the mountains floated all around, their perspective made fluid by sun and shadow; I remember the way the mountains dwarfed a deserted Ferris wheel in the Parque Nacional in late afternoon.

In fact the mountains loom behind every image I remember, and perhaps are themselves the connection. Some afternoons I would drive out along their talus slopes through the Chico district, out Carrera 7 where the grounds of the great houses were immaculately clipped and the gates bore brass plaques with the names of European embassies and American foundations and Argentinian neurologists. I recall stopping in El Chico to make a telephone call one day, from a small shopping center off Carrera 7; the shopping center adjoined a church where a funeral mass had just taken place. The mourners were leaving the church, talking on the street, the women, most of them, in black pant-suits and violet-tinted glasses and pleated silk dresses and Givenchy coats that had not been bought in Bogotá. In El Chico it did not seem so far to Paris or New York, but there remained the mountains, and beyond the mountains that dense world described by Gabriel García Márquez as so recent that many things lacked names.

And even just a little farther, out where Carrera 7 became the Carretera Central del Norte, the rutted road that plunged through the mountains to Tunja and eventually to Caracas, it was in many ways a perpetual frontier, vertiginous in its extremes. Rickety buses hurtled dizzyingly down the center of the road, swerving now and then to pick up a laborer, to avoid a pothole or a pack of children. Back from the road stretched large *haciendas,* their immense main houses barely visible in the folds of the slopes, their stone walls splashed occasionally with red paint, crude representations of the hammer and sickle and admonitions to vote *comunista.* One day when I was out there a cloud burst, and because my rented car with 110,000 miles on it had no windshield wipers, I stopped by the side of the road. Rain streamed over the MESA ARIZONA WESTWOOD WARRIORS and GO TIDE decals on the car windows. Gullies formed on the road. Up in the high gravel quarries men worked on, picking with shovels at the Andes for twelve and a half pesos a load.

Through another of our cities without a center, as hideous

as Los Angeles, and with as many cars
per head, and past the 20-foot neon sign
for Coppertone *on a church, past the population*
earning $700 per capita
in jerry skyscraper living-slabs, and on to the White
House
of El Presidente Leoni, his small men with 18-
inch repeating pistols, firing 45 bullets a minute,
the two armed guards petrified beside us, while we had
champagne,
and someone bugging the President: "Where are the
girls?"
And the enclosed leader, quite a fellow, saying,
"I don't know where yours are, but I know where to
find mine." . . .
This house, this pioneer democracy, built
on foundations, not of rock, but blood as hard as rock.
—Robert Lowell, "Caracas"

There is one more image I remember, and it comes in two parts. First there was the mine. Tunneled into a mountain in Zipaquirá, fifty kilometers north of Bogotá, is a salt mine. This single mine produces, each year, enough salt for all of South America, and has done so since before Europeans knew the continent existed: salt, not gold, was the economic basis of the Chibcha Empire, and Zipaquirá one of its capitals. The mine is vast, its air oppressive. I happened to be inside the mine because inside the mine there is, carved into the mountain 450 feet below the surface, a cathedral in which 10,000 people can hear mass at the same time. Fourteen massive stone pilasters support the vault. Recessed fluorescent tubes illuminate the Stations of the Cross, the dense air absorbing and dimming the light unsteadily. One could think of Chibcha sacrifices here, of the *conquistador* priests struggling to superimpose the European mass on the screams of the slaughtered children.

But one would be wrong. The building of this enigmatic excavation in the salt mountain was undertaken not by the Chibcha but by the Banco de la República, in 1954. In 1954 General Gustavo Rojas Pinilla and his colonels were running Colombia, and the country was wrenched by *La Violencia,* the fifteen years of anarchy that followed the assassination of Jorge Gaitán in Bogotá in 1948. In 1954 people were fleeing the terrorized countryside to squat in shacks in the comparative safety of Bogotá. In 1954 Colombia still had few public works projects, no transportation to speak of: Bogotá would not be connected by rail with the Caribbean until 1961. As I stood in the dim mountain reading the Banco de la República's dedicatory plaque, 1954 seemed to me an extraordinary year to have hit on the notion of building a cathedral of salt, but the Colombians to whom I mentioned it only shrugged.

The second part of the image. I had come up from the mine and was having lunch on the side of the salt mountain, in the chilly dining room of the Hostería del Libertador. There were heavy draperies that gave off a faint muskiness when touched. There were white brocade tablecloths, carefully darned. For every stalk of blanched asparagus served, there appeared another battery of silverplated flatware and platters and *vinaigrette* sauceboats, and also another battery of "waiters": little boys, twelve or thirteen years old, dressed in tailcoats and white gloves and taught to serve as if this small inn on an Andean precipice were Vienna under the Hapsburgs.

I sat there for a long time. All around us the wind was sweeping the clouds off the Andes and across the savannah. Four hundred and fifty feet beneath us was the cathedral built of salt in the year 1954. *This house, this pioneer democracy, built on foundations, not of rock, but blood as hard as rock.* One of the little boys in white gloves picked up an empty wine bottle from a table, fitted it precisely into a wine holder, and marched toward the kitchen holding it stiffly before him, glancing covertly at the *mâitre d'hôtel* for approval. It seemed to me later that I had never before seen and would perhaps never again see the residuum of European custom so movingly and pointlessly observed.

1974

At the Dam

Since the afternoon in 1967 when I first saw Hoover Dam, its image has never been entirely absent from my inner eye. I will be talking to someone in Los Angeles, say, or New York, and suddenly the dam will materialize, its pristine concave face gleaming white against the harsh rusts and taupes and mauves of that rock canyon hundreds or thousands of miles from where I am. I will be driving down Sunset Boulevard, or about to enter a freeway, and abruptly those power transmission towers will appear before me, canted vertiginously over the tailrace. Sometimes I am confronted by the intakes and sometimes by the shadow of the heavy cable that spans the canyon and sometimes by the ominous outlets to unused spillways, black in the lunar clarity of the desert light. Quite often I hear the turbines. Frequently I wonder what is happening at the dam this instant, at this precise intersection of time and space, how much water is being released to fill downstream orders and what lights are flashing and which generators are in full use and which just spinning free.

I used to wonder what it was about the dam that made me think of it at times and in places where I once thought of the Mindanao Trench, or of the stars wheeling in their courses, or of the words *As it was in the beginning, is now and ever shall be, world without end, amen*. Dams, after all, are commonplace: we have all seen one. This particular dam had existed as an idea in the world's mind for almost forty years before I saw it. Hoover Dam, showpiece of the Boulder Canyon project, the several million tons of concrete that made the Southwest plausible, the *fait accompli* that was to convey, in the innocent time of its construction, the notion that mankind's brightest promise lay in American engineering.

Of course the dam derives some of its emotional effect from precisely that aspect, that sense of being a monument to a faith since misplaced. "They died to make the desert bloom," reads a plaque dedicated to the 96 men who died building this first of the great high dams, and in context the worn phrase touches, suggests all of that trust in harnessing resources, in the meliorative power of the dynamo, so central to the early Thirties. Boulder City, built in 1931 as the construction town for the dam, retains the ambience of a model city, a new town, a toy triangular grid of green lawns and trim bungalows, all fanning out from the Reclamation building. The bronze sculptures at the dam itself evoke muscular citizens of a tomorrow that never came, sheaves of wheat clutched heavenward, thunderbolts defied. Winged Victories guard the flagpole. The flag whips in the canyon wind. An empty Pepsi-Cola can clatters across the terrazzo. The place is perfectly frozen in time.

But history does not explain it all, does not entirely suggest what makes that dam so affecting. Nor, even, does energy, the massive involvement with power and pressure and the transparent sexual overtones to that involvement. Once when I revisited the dam I walked through it with a man from the Bureau of Reclamation. For a while we trailed behind a guided tour, and then we went on, went into parts of the dam where visitors do not generally go. Once in a while he would explain something, usually in that recondite language having to do with "peaking power," with "outages" and "dewatering," but on the whole we spent the afternoon in a world so alien, so complete and so beautiful unto itself that it was scarcely necessary to speak at all. We saw almost no one. Cranes moved above us as if under their own volition. Generators roared. Transformers hummed. The gratings on which we stood vibrated. We watched a hundred-ton steel shaft plunging down to that place where the water was. And finally we got down to that place where the water was, where the water sucked out of Lake Mead roared through thirty-foot penstocks and then into thirteen-foot penstocks and finally into the turbines themselves. "Touch it," the Reclamation said, and I did, and for a long time I just stood there with my hands on the turbine. It was a peculiar moment, but so explicit as to suggest nothing beyond itself.

There was something beyond all that, something beyond energy, beyond history, something I could not fix in my mind. When I came up from the dam that day the wind was blowing harder, through the canyon and all across the Mojave. Later, toward Henderson and Las Vegas, there would be dust blowing, blowing past the Country-Western Casino FRI & SAT NITES and blowing past the Shrine of Our Lady of Safe Journey STOP & PRAY, but out at the dam there was no dust, only the rock and the dam and a little greasewood and a few garbage cans, their tops chained, banging against a fence. I walked across the marble star map that traces a sidereal revolution of the equinox and fixes forever, the Reclamation man had told me, for all time and for all people who can read the stars, the date the dam was dedicated. The star map was, he had said, for when we were all gone and the dam was left. I had not thought much of it when he said it, but I thought of it then, with the wind whining and the sun dropping behind a mesa with the finality of a sunset in space. Of course that was the image I had seen always, seen it without quite realizing what I saw, a dynamo finally free of man, splendid at last in its absolute isolation, transmitting power and releasing water to a world where no one is.

1970

V /

ON THE MORNING AFTER THE SIXTIES

On the Morning After the Sixties

I AM TALKING here about being a child of my time. When I think about the Sixties now I think about an afternoon not of the Sixties at all, an afternoon early in my sophomore year at Berkeley, a bright autumn Saturday in 1953. I was lying on a leather couch in a fraternity house (there had been a lunch for the alumni, my date had gone on to the game, I do not now recall why I had stayed behind), lying there alone reading a book by Lionel Trilling and listening to a middle-aged man pick out on a piano in need of tuning the melodic line to "Blue Room." All that afternoon he sat at the piano and all that afternoon he played "Blue Room" and he never got it right. I can hear and see it still, the wrong note in "We will thrive on / Keep alive on," the sunlight falling through the big windows, the man picking up his drink and beginning again and telling me, without ever saying a word, something I had not known before about bad marriages and wasted time and looking backward. That such an afternoon would now seem implausible in every detail—the idea of having had a "date" for a football lunch now seems to me so exotic as to be almost czarist—suggests the extent to which the narrative on which many of us grew up no longer applies.

The distance we have come from the world in which I went to college was on my mind quite a bit during those seasons when not only Berkeley but dozens of other campuses were periodically shut down, incipient battlegrounds, their borders sealed. To think of Berkeley as it was in the Fifties was not to think of barricades and reconstituted classes. "Reconstitution" would have sounded to us then like Newspeak, and barricades are never personal. We were all very personal then, sometimes relentlessly so, and, at that point where we either act or do not act, most of us are still. I suppose I am talking about just that: the ambiguity of belonging to a generation distrustful of political highs, the historical irrelevancy of growing up convinced that the heart of darkness lay not in some error of social organization but in man's own blood. If man was bound to err, then any social organization was bound to be in error. It was a premise which still seems to me accurate enough, but one which robbed us early of a certain capacity for surprise.

At Berkeley in the Fifties no one was surprised by anything at all, a *donnée* which tended to render discourse less than spirited, and debate nonexistent. The world was by definition imperfect, and so of course was the university. There was some talk even then about IBM cards, but on balance the notion that free education for tens of thousands of people might involve automation did not seem unreasonable. We took it for granted that the Board of Regents would sometimes act wrongly. We simply avoided those students rumored to be FBI informers. We were that generation called "silent," but we were silent neither, as some thought, because we shared the period's official optimism nor, as others thought, because we feared its official repression. We were silent because the exhilaration of social action seemed to many of us just one more way of escaping the personal, of masking for a while that dread of the meaningless which was man's fate.

To have assumed that particular fate so early was the peculiarity of my generation. I think now that we were the last generation to identify with adults. That most of us have found adulthood just as morally ambiguous as we expected it to be falls perhaps into the category of prophecies self-fulfilled: I am simply not sure. I am telling you only how it was. The mood of Berkeley in those years was one of mild but chronic "depression," against which I remember certain small things that seemed to me somehow explications, dazzling in their clarity, of the world I was about to enter: I remember a woman picking daffodils in the rain one day when I was walking in the hills. I remember a teacher who drank too much one night and revealed his fright and bitterness. I remember my real joy at discovering for the first time how language worked, at discovering, for example, that the central line of *Heart of Darkness* was a postscript. All such images were personal, and the personal was all that most of us expected to find. We would make a separate peace. We would do graduate work in Middle English, we would go abroad. We would make some money and live on a ranch. We would survive outside history, in a kind of *idée fixe* referred to always, during the years I spent at Berkeley, as "some little town with a decent beach."

As it worked out I did not find or even look for the little town with the decent beach. I sat in the large bare apartment in which I lived my junior and senior years (I had lived awhile in a sorority, the Tri Delt house, and had left it, typically, not over any "issue" but because I, the implacable "I," did not like living with sixty people) and I read Camus and Henry James and I watched a flowering plum come in and out of blossom and at night, most nights, I walked outside and looked up to where the cyclotron and the bevatron glowed on the dark hillside, unspeakable mysteries which engaged me, in the style of my time, only personally. Later I got out of Berkeley and went to New York and later I got out of New York and came to Los Angeles. What I have made for myself is personal, but is not exactly peace. Only one person I knew at Berkeley later discovered an ideology, dealt himself into history, cut himself loose from both his own dread and his own time. A few of the people I knew at Berkeley killed themselves not long after. Another attempted suicide in Mexico and then, in a recovery which seemed in many ways a more advanced derangement, came home and joined the Bank of America's three-year executive-training program. Most of us live less theatrically, but remain the survivors of a peculiar and inward time. If I could believe that going to a barricade would affect man's fate in the slightest I would go to that barricade, and quite often I wish that I could, but it would be less than honest to say that I expect to happen upon such a happy ending.

1970

Quiet Days in Malibu

1.

IN A WAY it seems the most idiosyncratic of beach communities, twenty-seven miles of coastline with no hotel, no passable restaurant, nothing to attract the traveler's dollar. It is not a resort. No one "vacations" or "holidays," as those words are conventionally understood, at Malibu. Its principal residential street, the Pacific Coast Highway, is quite literally a highway, California 1, which runs from the Mexican border to the Oregon line and brings Greyhound buses and refrigerated produce trucks and sixteen-wheel gasoline tankers hurtling past the front windows of houses frequently bought and sold for over a million dollars. The water off Malibu is neither as clear nor as tropically colored as the water off La Jolla. The beaches at Malibu are neither as white nor as wide as the beach at Carmel. The hills are scrubby and barren, infested with bikers and rattlesnakes, scarred with cuts and old burns and new R.V. parks. For these and other reasons Malibu tends to astonish and disappoint those who have never before seen it, and yet its very name remains, in the imagination of people all over the world, a kind of shorthand for the easy life. I had not before 1971 and will probably not again live in a place with a Chevrolet named after it.

2.

Dick Haddock, a family man, a man twenty-six years in the same line of work, a man who has on the telephone and in his office the crisp and easy manner of technological middle management, is in many respects the prototypical Southern California solid citizen. He lives in a San Fernando Valley subdivision near a freshwater marina and a good shopping plaza. His son is a high-school swimmer. His daughter is "into tennis." He drives thirty miles to and from work, puts in a forty-hour week, regularly takes courses to maintain his professional skills, keeps in shape and looks it. When he discusses his career he talks, in a kind of politely impersonal second person, about how "you would want like any other individual to advance yourself," about "improving your rating" and "being more of an asset to your department," about "really knowing your business." Dick Haddock's business for all these twenty-six years has been that of a professional lifeguard for the Los Angeles County Department of Beaches, and his office is a $190,000 lookout on Zuma Beach in northern Malibu.

It was Thanksgiving morning, 1975. A Santa Ana wind was just dying after blowing in off the Mojave for three weeks and setting 69,000 acres of Los Angeles County on fire. Squadrons of planes had been dropping chemicals on the fires to no effect. Querulous interviews with burned-out householders had become a fixed element of the six o'clock news. Smoke from the fires had that week stretched a hundred miles out over the Pacific and darkened the days and lit the nights and by Thanksgiving morning there was the sense all over Southern California of living in some grave solar dislocation. It was one of those weeks when Los Angeles seemed most perilously and breathtakingly itself, a cartoon of natural disaster, and it was a peculiar week in which to spend the day with Dick Haddock and the rest of the Zuma headquarters crew.

Actually I had wanted to meet the lifeguards ever since I moved to Malibu. I would drive past Zuma some cold winter mornings and see a few of them making their mandatory daily half-mile swims in open ocean. I would drive past Zuma some late foggy nights and see others moving around behind the lookout's lighted windows, the only other souls awake in all of northern Malibu. It seemed to me a curious, almost beatified career choice, electing to save those in peril upon the sea forty hours a week, and as the soot drifted down around the Zuma lookout on that Thanksgiving morning the laconic routines and paramilitary rankings of these civil servants in red trunks took on a devotionary and dreamlike inevitability. There was the "captain," John McFarlane, a man who had already taken his daily half-mile run and his daily half-mile swim and was putting on his glasses to catch up on paperwork. Had the water been below 56 degrees he would have been allowed to swim in a wet suit, but the water was not below 56 degrees and so he had swum as usual in his red trunks. The water was 58 degrees. John McFarlane is 48. There was the "lieutenant," Dick Haddock, telling me about how each of the Department's 125 permanent lifeguards (there are also 600 part-time or "recurrent" lifeguards) learns crowd control at the Los Angeles County Sheriff's Academy, learns emergency driving techniques at the California Highway Patrol

Academy, learns medical procedures at the U.S.C. Medical Center, and, besides running the daily half-mile and swimming the daily half-mile, does a monthly 500-meter paddle and a monthly pier jump. A "pier jump" is just what it sounds like, and its purpose is to gain practice around pilings in heavy surf.

There was as well the man out on patrol.

There were as well the "call-car personnel," two trained divers and cliff-climbers "ready to roll at any time" in what was always referred to as "a Code 3 vehicle with red light and siren," two men not rolling this Thanksgiving morning but sitting around the lookout, listening to the Los Angeles Rams beat the Detroit Lions on the radio, watching the gray horizon and waiting for a call.

No call came. The radios and the telephones crackled occasionally with reports from the other "operations" supervised by the Zuma crew: the "rescue-boat operation" at Paradise Cove, the "beach operations" at Leo Carrillo, Nicholas, Point Dume, Corral, Malibu Surfrider, Malibu Lagoon, Las Tunas, Topanga North and Topanga South. Those happen to be the names of some Malibu public beaches but in the Zuma lookout that day the names took on the sound of battle stations during a doubtful cease-fire. All quiet at Leo. Situation normal at Surfrider.

The lifeguards seemed most comfortable when they were talking about "operations" and "situations," as in "a phone-watch situation" or "a riptide situation." They also talked easily about "functions," as in "the function of maintaining a secure position on the beach." Like other men at war they had charts, forms, logs, counts kept current to within twelve hours: *1405 surf rescues off Zuma between 12:01 A.M. January 1, 1975 and 11:59 P.M. Thanksgiving Eve 1975.* As well as: *36,120 prevention rescues, 872 first aids, 176 beach emergency calls, 12 resuscitations, 8 boat distress calls, 107 boat warnings, 438 lost-and-found children,* and *0 deaths.* Zero. No body count. When he had occasion to use the word "body" Dick Haddock would hesitate and glance away.

On the whole the lifeguards favored a diction as flat and finally poetic as that of Houston Control. Everything that morning was "real fine." The headquarters crew was "feeling good." The day was "looking good." Malibu surf was "two feet and shape is poor." Earlier that morning there had been a hundred or so surfers in the water, a hundred or so of those bleached children of indeterminate age and sex who bob off Zuma and appear to exist exclusively on packaged beef jerky, but by ten they had all pocketed their Thanksgiving jerky and moved on to some better break. "It heats up, we could use some more personnel," Dick Haddock said about noon, assessing the empty guard towers. "That happened, we might move on a decision to open Towers One and Eleven, I'd call and say we need two recurrents at Zuma, plus I might put an extra man at Leo."

It did not heat up. Instead it began to rain, and on the radio the morning N.F.L. game gave way to the afternoon N.F.L. game, and after a while I drove with one of the call-car men to Paradise Cove, where the rescue-boat crew needed a diver. They did not need a diver to bring up a body, or a murder weapon, or a crate of stolen ammo, or any of the things Department divers sometimes get their names in the paper for bringing up. They needed a diver, with scuba gear and a wet suit, because they had been removing the propeller from the rescue boat and had dropped a metal part the size of a dime in twenty feet of water. I had the distinct impression that they particularly needed a diver in a wet suit because nobody on the boat crew wanted to go back in the water in his trunks to replace the propeller, but there seemed to be some tacit agreement that the lost part was to be considered the point of the dive.

"I guess you know it's fifty-eight down there," the diver said.

"Don't need to tell me how cold it is," the boat lieutenant said. His name was Leonard McKinley and he had "gone permanent" in 1942 and he was of an age to refer to Zuma as a "bathing" beach. "After you find that little thing you could put the propeller back on for us, you wanted. As long as you're in the water anyway? In your suit?"

"I had a feeling you'd say that."

Leonard McKinley and I stood on the boat and watched the diver disappear. In the morning soot from the fires had coated the surface but now the wind was up and the soot was clouding the water. Kelp fronds undulated on the surface. The boat rocked. The radio sputtered with reports of a yacht named *Ursula* in distress.

"One of the other boats is going for it," Leonard McKinley said. "We're not. Some days we just sit here like firemen. Other days, a day with rips, I been out ten hours straight. You get your big rips in the summer, swells coming up from Mexico. A Santa Ana, you get your capsized boats, we got one the other day, it was overdue out of Santa Monica, they were about drowned when we picked them up."

I tried to keep my eyes on the green-glass water but could not. I had been sick on boats in the Catalina Channel and in the Gulf of California and even in San

Francisco Bay, and now I seemed to be getting sick on a boat still moored at the end of the Paradise Cove pier. The radio reported the *Ursula* under tow to Marina del Rey. I concentrated on the pilings.

"He gets the propeller on," Leonard McKinley said, "you want to go out?"

I said I thought not.

"You come back another day," Leonard McKinley said, and I said that I would, and although I have not gone back there is no day when I do not think of Leonard McKinley and Dick Haddock and what they are doing, what situations they face, what operations, what green-glass water. The water today is 56 degrees.

3.

AMADO VAZQUEZ is a Mexican national who has lived in Los Angeles County as a resident alien since 1947. Like many Mexicans who have lived for a long time around Los Angeles he speaks of Mexico as "over there," remains more comfortable in Spanish than in English, and transmits, in his every movement, a kind of "different" propriety, a correctness, a cultural reserve. He is in no sense a Chicano. He is rather what California-born Mexicans sometimes call "Mexican-from-Mexico," pronounced as one word and used to suggest precisely that difference, that rectitude, that personal conservatism. He was born in Ahualulco, Jalisco. He was trained as a barber at the age of ten. Since the age of twenty-seven, when he came north to visit his brother and find new work for himself, he has married, fathered two children, and become, to the limited number of people who know and understand the rather special work he found for himself in California, a kind of legend. Amado Vazquez was, at the time I first met him, head grower at Arthur Freed Orchids, a commercial nursery in Malibu founded by the late motion-picture producer Arthur Freed, and he is one of a handful of truly great orchid breeders in the world.

In the beginning I met Amado Vazquez not because I knew about orchids but because I liked greenhouses. All I knew about orchids was that back in a canyon near my house someone was growing them *in greenhouses*. All I knew about Amado Vazquez was that he was the man who would let me spend time alone in these greenhouses. To understand how extraordinary this seemed to me you would need to have craved the particular light and silence of greenhouses as I did: all my life I had been trying to spend time in one greenhouse or another, and all my life the person in charge of one greenhouse or another had been trying to hustle me out. When I was nine I would deliberately miss the school bus in order to walk home, because by walking I could pass a greenhouse. I recall being told at that particular greenhouse that the purchase of a nickel pansy did not entitle me to "spend the day," and at another that my breathing was "using up the air."

And yet back in this canyon near my house twenty-five years later were what seemed to me the most beautiful greenhouses in the world—the most aqueous filtered light, the softest tropical air, the most silent clouds of flowers—and the person in charge, Amado Vazquez, seemed willing to take only the most benign notice of my presence. He seemed to assume that I had my own reasons for being there. He would speak only to offer a nut he had just cracked, or a flower cut from a plant he was pruning. Occasionally Arthur

Freed's brother Hugo, who was then running the business, would come into the greenhouse with real customers, serious men in dark suits who appeared to have just flown in from Taipei or Durban and who spoke in hushed voices, as if they had come to inspect medieval enamels, or uncut diamonds.

But then the buyers from Taipei or Durban would go into the office to make their deal and the silence in the greenhouse would again be total. The temperature was always 72 degrees. The humidity was always 60 per cent. Great arcs of white phalaenopsis trembled overhead. I learned the names of the crosses by studying labels there in the greenhouse, the exotic names whose value I did not then understand. *Amabilis* × *Rimestadiana* = *Elisabethae*. *Aphrodite* × *Rimestadiana* = *Gilles Gratiot*. *Amabilis* × *Gilles Gratiot* = *Katherine Siegwart* and *Katherine Siegwart* × *Elisabethae* = *Doris*. *Doris* after Doris Duke. *Doris* which first flowered at Duke Farms in 1940. At least once each visit I would remember the nickel pansy and find Amado Vazquez and show him a plant I wanted to buy, but he would only smile and shake his head. "For breeding," he would say, or "not for sale today." And then he would lift the spray of flowers and show me some point I would not have noticed, some marginal difference in the substance of the petal or the shape of the blossom. "Very beautiful," he would say. "Very nice you like it." What he would not say was that these plants he was letting me handle, these plants "for breeding" or "not for sale today," were stud plants, and that the value of such a plant at Arthur Freed could range from ten thousand to more than three-quarters of a million dollars.

I suppose the day I realized this was the day I stopped using the Arthur Freed greenhouses as a place to eat my lunch, but I made a point of going up one day in 1976 to see Amado Vazquez and to talk to Marvin Saltzman, who took over the business in 1973 and is married to Arthur Freed's daughter Barbara. (As in *Phal. Barbara Freed Saltzman* "Jean McPherson," *Phal. Barbara Freed Saltzman* "Zuma Canyon," and *Phal. Barbara Freed Saltzman* "Malibu Queen," three plants "not for sale today" at Arthur Freed.) It was peculiar talking to Marvin Saltzman because I had never before been in the office at Arthur Freed, never seen the walls lined with dulled silver awards, never seen the genealogical charts on the famous Freed hybrids, never known anything at all about the actual business of orchids.

"Frankly it's an expensive business to get into," Marvin Saltzman said. He was turning the pages of *Sander's List*, the standard orchid studbook, published every several years and showing the parentage of every hybrid registered with the Royal Horticultural Society, and he seemed oblivious to the primeval silence of the greenhouse beyond the office window. He had shown me how Amado Vazquez places the pollen from one plant into the ovary of a flower on another. He had explained that the best times to do this are at full moon and high tide, because phalaenopsis plants are more fertile then. He had explained that a phalaenopsis is more fertile at full moon because in nature it must be pollinated by a night-flying moth, and over sixty-five million years of evolution its period of highest fertility began to coincide with its period of highest visibility. He had explained that a phalaenopsis is more fertile at high tide because the moisture content of every plant responds to tidal movement. It was all an old story to Marvin Saltzman. I could not take my eyes from the window.

"You bring back five thousand seedlings from the jungle and you wait three years for them to flower," Marvin Saltzman said. "You find two you like and you throw out the other four thousand nine hundred ninety-eight and you try to breed the two. Maybe the pollenization takes, eighty-five per cent of the time it doesn't. Say you're lucky, it takes, you'll still wait another four years before you see a flower. Meanwhile you've got a big capital investment. An Arthur Freed could take $400,000 a year from M-G-M and put $100,000 of it into getting this place started, but not many people could. You see a lot of what we call backyard nurseries—people who have fifty or a hundred plants, maybe they have two they think are exceptional, they decide to breed them—but you talk about major nurseries, there are maybe only ten in the United States, another ten in Europe. That's about it. Twenty."

Twenty is also about how many head growers there are, which is part of what lends Amado Vazquez his legendary aspect, and after a while I left the office and went out to see him in the greenhouse. There in the greenhouse everything was operating as usual to approximate that particular level of a Malaysian rain forest—not on the ground but perhaps a hundred feet up—where epiphytic orchids grow wild. In the rain forest these orchids get broken by wind and rain. They get pollinated randomly and rarely by insects. Their seedlings are crushed by screaming monkeys and tree boas and the orchids live unseen and die young. There in the greenhouse nothing would break the orchids and they would be pollinated at full moon and high tide by Amado Vazquez, and their seedlings would be tended in a sterile box with sterile gloves and sterile tools by Amado Vazquez's wife, Maria, and the orchids would not seem to die at all. "We don't know how long they'll live," Marvin Saltzman told me. "They haven't been bred under protected conditions that long. The botanists estimate a hundred and fifty, two hundred years, but we don't know. All we know is that a plant a hundred years old will show no signs of senility."

It was very peaceful there in the greenhouse with Amado Vazquez and the plants that would outlive us both. "We grew in osmunda then," he said suddenly. Osmunda is a potting medium. Amado Vazquez talks exclusively in terms of how the orchids grow. He had been talking about the years when he first came to this country and got a job with his brother tending a private orchid collection in San Marino, and he had fallen silent. "I didn't know orchids then, now they're like my children. You wait for the first bloom like you wait for a baby to come. Sometimes you wait four years and it opens and it isn't what you expected, maybe your heart wants to break, but you love it. You never say, 'that one was prettier.' You just love them. My whole life is orchids."

And in fact it was. Amado Vazquez's wife, Maria (as in *Phal. Maria Vasquez* "Malibu," the spelling of Vazquez being mysteriously altered by everyone at Arthur Freed except the Vazquezes themselves), worked in the laboratory at Arthur Freed. His son, George (as in *Phal. George Vasquez* "Malibu"), was the sales manager at Arthur Freed. His daughter, Linda (as in *Phal. Linda Mia* "Innocence"), worked at Arthur Freed before her marriage. Amado Vazquez will often get up in the night to check a heater, adjust a light, hold a seed pod in his hand and try to sense if morning will be time enough to sow the seeds in the sterile flask. When Amado and Maria Vazquez go to Central or South

America, they go to look for orchids. When Amado and Maria Vazquez went for the first time to Europe a few years ago, they looked for orchids. "I asked all over Madrid for orchids," Amado Vazquez recalled. "Finally they tell me about this one place. I go there, I knock. The woman finally lets me in. She agrees to let me see the orchids. She takes me into a house and . . ."

Amado Vazquez broke off, laughing.

"She has three orchids," he finally managed to say. "Three. One of them dead. All three from Oregon."

We were standing in a sea of orchids, an extravagance of orchids, and he had given me an armful of blossoms from his own cattleyas to take to my child, more blossoms maybe than in all of Madrid. It seemed to me that day that I had never talked to anyone so direct and unembarrassed about the things he loved. He had told me earlier that he had never become a United States citizen because he had an image in his mind which he knew to be false but could not shake: the image was that of standing before a judge and stamping on the flag of Mexico. "And I love my country," he had said. Amado Vazquez loved his country. Amado Vazquez loved his family. Amado Vazquez loved orchids. "You want to know how I feel about the plants," he said as I was leaving. "I'll tell you. I will die in orchids."

4.

IN THE PART of Malibu where I lived from January of 1971 until quite recently we all knew one another's cars, and watched for them on the highway and at the

Trancas Market and at the Point Dume Gulf station. We exchanged information at the Trancas Market. We left packages and messages for one another at the Gulf station. We called one another in times of wind and fire and rain, we knew when one another's septic tanks needed pumping, we watched for ambulances on the highway and helicopters on the beach and worried about one another's dogs and horses and children and corral gates and Coastal Commission permits. An accident on the highway was likely to involve someone we knew. A rattlesnake in my driveway meant its mate in yours. A stranger's campfire on your beach meant fire on both our slopes.

In fact this was a way of life I had not expected to find in Malibu. When I first moved in 1971 from Hollywood to a house on the Pacific Coast Highway I had accepted the conventional notion that Malibu meant the easy life, had worried that we would be cut off from "the real world," by which I believe I meant daily exposure to the Sunset Strip. By the time we left Malibu, seven years later, I had come to see the spirit of the place as one of shared isolation and adversity, and I think now that I never loved the house on the Pacific Coast Highway more than on those many days when it was impossible to leave it, when fire or flood had in fact closed the highway. We moved to this house on the highway in the year of our daughter's fifth birthday. In the year of her twelfth it rained until the highway collapsed, and one of her friends drowned at Zuma Beach, a casualty of Quaaludes.

One morning during the fire season of 1978, some months after we had sold the house on the Pacific Coast Highway, a brush fire caught in Agoura, in the San Fernando Valley. Within two hours a Santa Ana wind had pushed this fire across 25,000 acres and thirteen miles to the coast, where it jumped the Pacific Coast Highway as a half-mile fire storm generating winds of 100 miles per hour and temperatures up to 2500 degrees Fahrenheit. Refugees huddled on Zuma Beach. Horses caught fire and were shot on the beach, birds exploded in the air. Houses did not explode but imploded, as in a nuclear strike. By the time this fire storm had passed 197 houses had vanished into ash, many of them houses which belonged or had belonged to people we knew. A few days after the highway reopened I drove out to Malibu to see Amado Vazquez, who had, some months before, bought from the Freed estate all the stock at Arthur Freed Orchids, and had been in the process of moving it a half-mile down the canyon to his own new nursery, Zuma Canyon Orchids. I found him in the main greenhouse at what had been Arthur Freed Orchids. The place was now a range not of orchids but of shattered glass and melted metal and the imploded shards of the thousands of chemical beakers that had held the Freed seedlings, the new crosses. "I lost three years," Amado Vazquez said, and for an instant I thought we would both cry. "You want today to see flowers," he said then, "we go down to the other place." I did not want that day to see flowers. After I said goodbye to Amado Vazquez my husband and daughter and I went to look at the house on the Pacific Coast Highway in which we had lived for seven years. The fire had come to within 125 feet of the property, then stopped or turned or been beaten back, it was hard to tell which. In any case it was no longer our house.

1976–1978